The Subconscious Door to Wealth

Verses Kindler Publication

VERSES KINDLER PUBLICATION

Verses Kindler Publication.

Website: www.verseskindlerpublication.com

The Subconscious Door to Wealth

By: Mr. Patrick Johnson

ISBN: 978-93-5605-531-5

FICTION STORIES 1st Edition

Price: 249 INR/$12

VERSES KINDLER PUBLICATION

DISCLAIMER

Chapter 1: Fanning the Flame in Your Subconscious

The power of the burning desire and its influence on the subconscious mind.

"Desire is the starting point of all achievement, not a hope, not a wish, but a keen pulsating desire which transcends everything." How does one transcend disadvantaged beginnings or daunting obstacles to achieve great success? The formula often contains one essential ingredient: an unrelenting, all-consuming desire that dominates the subconscious mind.

Consider the story of Reginald Lewis. Lewis was born poor in 1942 in a Baltimore neighborhood rampant with racism and lack of opportunity. His father worked as a laborer in a shipyard while his mother took care of Reginald and his four siblings in their small rowhouse apartment. From an early age, Lewis possessed a fiery determination not just to climb the ladder of success but also to eventually own the entire ladder company. Growing up, Lewis faced discrimination and had minimal financial resources to support his dreams of becoming a successful businessman and a lawyer. But nothing could deter his internal compass oriented singularly towards triumph against the odds.

To fund his education, Lewis worked two or three minimum wage jobs at a time - from construction worker to postal employee to dance instructor - while excelling academically. He graduated with honors from Virginia State College in 1965. He enrolled at Harvard Law School that fall, becoming the only student in the history of 148 years who was admitted before applying. After earning his law degree, Lewis broke racial barriers on Wall Street by securing a position as an associate attorney at one of New York's oldest and most prestigious corporate law firms. But

Lewis knew that his burning desire would only be satisfied when he owned his own company.

In 1987, Lewis acquired the failing Beatrice International Foods using creative financing methods despite naysayers claiming that no bank would finance a leveraged buyout for a Black businessman. Over the next five years, through visionary leadership and strategic expansion, Lewis transformed Beatrice into the first Black-owned billion-dollar business in the U.S. Even today, over 25 years later, Lewis remains an icon of subconscious success and the power of desires turned conviction.

What fueled Lewis' extraordinary rise? Sheer willpower and unshakable belief in his eventual success despite little external evidence initially to support it. Lewis inhabited a reality in his mind where obstacles simply did not exist. Though far from inevitable or easy, his path to victory was assured - he merely had to put one foot determinedly in front of the other until the finish line. Lewis attributed this "desire so strong that it becomes an obsession" as the indispensable guiding force, making the improbable inevitable. As Lewis put it, **"Make up your mind that you are going to be rich...You have to believe it so strongly, so absolutely, that you can see it, touch it, smell it, taste it. It drives everything you do."**

This chapter explores how to fan the flames of an all-encompassing desire into an obsession and channel its power to dominate your subconscious mind. This internal focus sparks external manifestation. Modeling mentors like Reginald Lewis, who traversed vast distances between poverty and wealth, can illuminate the way forward. The principles we will cover include:

Developing a soul-consuming drive oriented solely toward success

Feed this drive daily through creative visualization, affirmations, and immersion in your aims. Model the habits and mindsets of ultra-achievers. Let ambition course through your veins and persist no matter what surface obstacles arise. Reflect often on your burning desire and its achievement as an established fact cemented in your mind.

For example, from childhood, Lewis determined that his purpose was to excel academically, dominate the business world, and never accept less than his envisioned reality out of a poverty mindset. No matter the difficulty of his daily grind, working multiple jobs while in school full-time, Lewis maintained this mental picture of destined victory. He awoke early, went to bed late, and devoted all spare minutes and moments to affirmations, business plan development, and activities furthering his single-minded ambition.

Tapping Into Your Primal Purpose

Before we dive further, it is essential to address a crucial foundation - purpose. What for you is this burning desire for material wealth that fuels itself? At its core, ambition arises from purpose. We all possess deeply rooted reasons for being - primal passions and talents meant for expression in this life. Connecting to your unique purpose fuels the flames that drive subconscious potential to manifest.

Consider technology visionary Steve Jobs, Oprah Winfrey, and civil rights activist Dr. Martin Luther King Jr. Early on; they discovered core themes, messages, and disciplines toward which they channeled ambition. Each is history-altering in impact. Their life visions arose from purpose first, then spread fire outward.

Ask yourself: Why choose wealth over other pursuits? How specifically will fortunes financially fulfill a broader purpose? Lewis grew up underprivileged, so economics meant access. He secured wealth to support African Americans' education/entrepreneurship and operationalize equality. Wealth, for wealth's sake, never sustains drive when obstacles arise. Purpose-born passion does.

Clarity of purpose also eliminates internal conflict bred by competing interests that suffocate drive. Lewis said no to umpteen opportunities to remain focused on his law firm and then acquisition trajectories. **"I wanted to build something that was quite different from what my classmates were talking about,"** Lewis attested, **"going to work for a law firm, becoming a partner...I knew basically what I wanted to do, and I was one hell of a guy with blinders on."**

Four techniques for discovering your primal purpose:

1) Childhood Analysis: What originally inspired your imagination and filled hours of concentration? What talents and topics ignited your early interests? Revisit old visions through that lens of meaning.

2) Value Excavation: Consider your core values - what principles guide your life ethos? Do specific issues consistently stir your emotions? Why? Dig there.

3) Thought Harvesting: Over the next month, record stray thoughts, mini-ideas, and visions that randomly arise. Detect patterns pointing to purpose.

4) If Anything Were Possible: Hypothesize without any limits on time, money, or obligations. What pursuits call you? Why so meaningful?

Once your purpose flames arise, all else effortlessly flows. **"There's nothing enlightened about shrinking so that other people won't feel insecure around you,"** declared Lewis.

Harnessing emotions to fuel your subconscious capacity

Emotionally charge your thoughts and visions related to your quest. Feel what it would be like to obtain your ambitious objectives already. When Lewis pictured his future billion-dollar deal, he immersed himself in the emotional state of triumph, pride in ownership, and relief at securing financial freedom for his family. He fused those feelings deeply into his mental creation process to manifest that exact vision externally later in life. You, too, must feel the fire of desire, not just think it!

Channeling imagination to create a detailed mental blueprint

Envision precisely the outcome wanted as if it exists now with full sensory engagement. What do you see, hear, feel, smell, and taste when inhabiting this reality where your bold aspirations are fulfilled? Lewis conducted visualizations where he saw himself as head of a prosperous multinational conglomerate. He walked through his modern skyscraper headquarters overseeing new business ventures, smelled the leather seat in his luxury vehicle as he visited factories, and tasted victory sipping champagne while toasting his IPO. Constructing this mental palace in minute detail provided a clear trajectory for Lewis' subconscious creation. **"Don't build your dreams on concrete; build dreams in your mind's eye,"** Liz Armbruster wrote. Vivid mental creation provides trajectories for realization.

Now let's explore practical steps for living these principles:

Develop Your Inner Drive

Upon waking, voice 3 desire statements:
- "I am deeply passionate about [X]."
- "My willpower is unmatched; I persevere amidst all storms."

- "Through committed purpose & self-mastery, I manifest my destiny."

Create vision boards with images, phrases, and quotes evoking your burning ambition. Display them prominently.

Emotionally Charge Your Subconscious

Meditate on desire fulfillment for 5-10 minutes daily. Use all senses. Feel rewards deeply, eliciting physiological responses.

Write "Victory Journal" entries detailing succeeding on meaningful goals as if they happened already. Savor your emotions; be specific.

Construct Mental Blueprints

Script an "Ideal Day" visualization outlining your perfect day in detail once ambitious desires are realized. Visualize frequently.

Storyboard your future using sketches of critical scenes - acquiring a company, moving into a dream home. Add descriptive narrative.

Master these principles to fan your internal fire and powerfully program your subconscious. Ignite purpose, energy, and emotion into mental movie reels compiled consistently and creativity. Mindset shifts Manifest. Desires transferred to become a reality. Blaze forth unstoppably!

The consuming fire of Lewis' desire functioned as the North Star guiding him through all storms toward his destiny of riches and ownership. He saw himself as triumphant, so external setbacks only fueled his internal flame. When a business loan application got rejected, Lewis likely affirmed to himself: **"I am the captain**

of my ship, the master of my soul." He believed unconditionally in his eventual success.

You, too, can fan desire's fire and channel its power to manifest reality. The fuel lies within. **"Don't wish it was easier; wish you were better. Don't wish for fewer problems; wish for more skills. Don't wish for less challenges; wish for more wisdom,"** reflects the mindset Lewis embodied. Continually feed your burning desire not through wishing but through skilled subconscious programming and bold visionary action.

The journey begins now in the subconscious depths where bold visions ignite. Construct your mental palace brick by brick until you inhabit its rooms in your mind's eye. Walk through the hallways with the assurance that your desires will soon materialize externally. **"The mind is everything. What you think you become,"** Buddha taught. Your belief molds reality.

Fan your flames higher through obsessive desire and emotional conviction. Let ambitious imagination consume conscious thought. Manifest the future now before it births itself. Center your subconscious on what you believe, desire, and envision, not external constraints. **"You are essentially who you create yourself to be, and all that occurs in your life is the result of your own making,"** Lewis counseled. May these sparks kindle your fire as they did his own. Let the flames rise!

The skies now set no limit on your yearnings. Unleash the endless power within to claim your kingdom. Glory awaits those whose desire masters all. Destiny calls - dare you answer? Fan the flames until they burn bright for all to see. Our light can blind those without such desire's fire blazing within their soul. Blaze on, my friend, blaze on until the Earth itself awakens to your glow!

Chapter 2: Belief as the Pillar for Subconscious Success

The role of faith in subconscious mind programming for success

"Doubt creates complications; faith allows you to realize simplicity." The previous chapter emphasized stoking up internal desire, which can act as an impetus for the subconscious mind and manifest capabilities. Nevertheless, desire is not sufficient to modify the reality we live in. To sustain those inner flames within, you need one essential thing—unfailing belief—in yourself and your visions despite shallow processes.

Martin Luther King Jr. perfectly illustrates that if you have the right amount of conviction and confidence, you can accomplish something greater than what people might think is impossible. He was an African American minister who lived during the 1950s, which happened to be the worst period when it came to racism, oppression, and all sorts of injustices. Racism and discrimination sat like ironclads in the face of people's prayers of having a community of equal people.

However, King was deeply convinced that this outrageous imbalance between injustice and justice would, someday, be increasingly torn down to make space for a redefined world. He envisioned a nation where all people were united, judged not **"by the colour of their skin but by the content of their character."** King held firm to his belief in this moral vision despite its current societal absence.

What gave this solitary Southern preacher the power to catalyze dismantling institutionalized injustice? Quite simply, it is an unyielding belief. King's faith saturated his subconscious mind with unshakable determination that equality's inevitability was more accurate than any outward dismissiveness or danger.

"Faith is taking the first step, even when you don't see the whole staircase."

So when confronted by snarling mobs, brutal police assaults, jail terms, church bombings, and assassination attempts, King's internal belief system remained resolute and imperturbable as granite. **"We've got some difficult days ahead," he admitted with preternatural calm. "But it really doesn't matter with me now because I've been to the mountaintop...And I've looked over and seen the Promised Land."**

King's soul was subconsciously programmed with the certainty of his righteous cause's triumph. No vicious hecklers, governing edicts, or violent attacks could extinguish the brilliant luminescence he held firmly in his mind's eye. That sustaining internal light eventually radiated outward, galvanizing a movement and illuminating all of America. **"An individual has not started living until he can rise above the narrow confines of his individualistic concerns to the broader concerns of all humanity,"** reflected King. His impassioned belief manifested historic justice in the Civil Rights Act of 1964 and the Voting Rights Act of 1965 after years of mass protests, boycotts, and jailings. King's transcendent dream became a tangible reality.

Like desire's flames, personal belief is essential for transforming aspirations from fantasies into forthcoming facts. As King remarked, **"The future you envision is the future you will inherit."** Undergirding your ambitions with steadfast faith allows the subconscious mind to operate with supreme confidence. It infuses thoughts and visualizations from a foundation of intrinsic certitude in their manifesting power. Sustainable belief provides the potent energizing force to persevere undeterred despite any impediments arising.

Adopting the empowered mindset of a "believer" involves deeply embodying tenets of:

Affirmation: Believing something is yours through affirmative assertion despite temporary outer appearances. King constantly affirmed liberty's coming hour through speeches, writings, and everyday mantras. **"We shall overcome because the arc of the moral universe is long, but it bends towards justice."**

Visualization: Conditioning your mind's eye with vivid multi-sensory impressions of your visions being fulfilled. King immersed himself in future freedom celebrations—the thunderous sounds of cheering crowds, joyful sights of interracial families embracing, and raw embodied exhilaration as injustice crumbled.

Acting "As If": Carrying yourself with standards and behaviours befitting the person and reality you believe represents your inevitable future manifestation. King conveyed himself with dignity, befitting the just society he prophesied himself to be. He then imbued those same empowered mindsets of deserved equality into his millions of followers.

Positive Self-Talk: Implanting your consciousness with encouraging optimism and affirmative counterpoints to any insecurity or doubts. King maintained an uplifting focus and a calming internal narrative that his morally righteous cause would prevail. **"We must accept finite disappointment but never lose infinite hope."**

Emotional Investment: Allowing oneself to experience the visceral feelings associated with your realized vision daily. Adding impassioned intensity magnifies tangible manifesting impacts. King exuded emotional conviction when tearfully pleading, **"I have a dream!"** - a call that became the Civil Rights Movement's soaring rallying cry. It awakened and galvanized the collective American soul to rise.

Carefully cultivated belief systems catalyze the metaphysical alchemy of transforming unformed potential into manifested creation. Belief makes the subconscious mind an invaluable collaborator, not an adversary, in your realization. This inner plane of thought, emotion, and focused visualization simply follows the highly charged belief instructions you supply as its animating source code.

Will your dominant subconscious programming reflect beliefs in abundance, love, and success, or limiting mindsets of lack, fear, and anxiety? Your core beliefs represent the bedrock upon which any ambitions are erected.

As Napoleon Hill famously asserted: **"Whatever the mind can conceive and believe, it can achieve."** Master empowered belief, and the subconscious will ensure your "wildest visions" manifestation into tangible reality. Belief is the mechanism rendering perceived boundaries limitless. Adopt an audaciously optimistic certitude in yourself and bear witness as the universe realigns to follow your convictions obediently.

Yet crucially, transformative sustainable belief should never blind itself with empty words, confessions, or rhetorical artifice. Instead, like King's movement, it begins in humble transcendental quietude - the still depths within each soul listening keenly for life's deafening existential whispers amidst superficial noise. **"Faith is the substance of things hoped for, the evidence of things not seen" - it subsists in realms beyond surface phenomena.**

Four Pathways to Cultivating Empowered Belief:

1) Purpose-Rooting Your Beliefs

Clarity of inspired overarching purpose uproots internal conflicts and competing interests that breed self-doubt. Martin Luther

King Jr.'s incandescent beliefs were grounded in his spiritual calling to uplift oppressed communities through enacting God's moral justice and equity on Earth. His "why" provided supreme meaning, infusing fervour into convictions.

What is your defining life purpose fueling beliefs? Root them in your deepest personal mythos, the origins and symbolism of your narrative self-actualization journey. A clearly defined motivating "why" magnetizes all minor doubts into a singularity of powerful unified focus.

Insecurity often arises from a lack of authentically reinforcing values undergirding one's beliefs. But with purpose as a crystal primal guiding force, beliefs become simplified by singular consecration to what truly matters most. Doubt and fear are subconscious manifestations of murky prioritization. Cement your core values, and divine will float your ship's sails via self-belief.

2) Testing Belief Through Action

While philosophical introspection plants the seeds of belief, consistent concrete action allows those seeds to germinate, blossom, and eventually bear fruit into empowered mindsets. Each endeavor you successfully complete stands as an embodied affirmation of your identity's transformation, reflecting who you believe yourself to become. Victories compound self-belief.

King mounted civil disobedience campaigns that withstood fire hoses, attack dogs, and hate-filled derision to expand belief in their validity despite sceptics' mockery. The belief multiplied exponentially with each subsequent reinforcing boycott, march, and incremental legislative win accomplished. Start proving self-beliefs in low-stakes areas to fortify confidence before scaling up ambitions. Let each small victory fan flames.

3) Optimize Your Belief Environment

To bolster beliefs into imperturbable bedrock convictions, surround your daily existence with inspiring totems embodying your paramount ideals. Consciously architect your living/work spaces with belief-conditioning multimedia experiences designed to reshape attitudes iteratively.

King's team meticulously crafted their headquarters campus into a total belief immersion. Every wall showcased affirmational quotes, inspirational artwork celebrating human dignity, and constant audio/visual reminders highlighting the movement's moral urgency. Environment programs cognition. As decades of marketing psychology attests, external stimuli shape internal thought.

Construct a "belief-augmented reality" encompassing every sensory element of your aesthetic milieu. Transform each sight, sound, and tactile impression into confirmation of the future ideal you inhabit. Let no corner remain neutral—claim all environmental stimuli as reconditioning regimens. Treat surrounding spaces as conscious physical embodiments of your idealized destiny.

You can only merge self and environment into one unified, empowered experience. Your mindsets and mental models alter your surroundings as they evolve. An ouroboros of infinite progress birthing gods.

4) Inculcating "Growth Mindset" - Fluent Belief Evolution

Embed mental tenets of continual education, limitation-defiance, and positively perseverant thinking into your beliefs' core architecture. Uphold affirmations like: **"If you can't fly, run; If you can't run, walk; If you can't walk, crawl. But by all**

means, keep moving!" Beliefs must remain ever-evolving spiritual practices versus rigid dogmas.

The human brain has evolved to make continuous sense of virtually any information, whether reliable or misleading. Let this first software program perform a never-ending loop of self-healing and enhancement. Be a continuous wonder in a never-ending world of paradigms. Take on life as a little acolyte with pure receptiveness to develop human understanding through daily lived experiences.

Do not fear "failures"—try to grab them as quick lessons on your way to success. Humblely embrace each fall as a tribute to expensive lessons devoted to honed self-mastery. However, there is no enlightenment in shrinking so as not to intimidate other people. Reginald Lewis aptly captured this Statement.

Only fixed thoughts that dictate people to oppose can create doubt. The growth-oriented thinking approach provides an unwavering determination that comes from supernatural experience. There is no reason to stop pushing boundaries. As King reminded us, **"We are not makers of history. We are made by history."** Grander visions beckon beyond the horizon!

The empowered personality is a skilful mason strategically constructing dominant belief systems as mankind's most powerful technology for subconscious mastery over physical reality. You, too, can command this godlike ability by imprinting foundational paramount beliefs that propel you towards greatness.

Focus intently on identifying what empowering beliefs, once embedded as your prevailing philosophies, would radically restructure your material circumstances. Vividly envision your wealthiest, fittest, most actualized being. Who does that individual believe themselves to be? What principles and convictions do they uncompromisingly uphold?

Concentrate fully on inhabiting that internal ideal - their electrifying presence, razor-sharp confidence, and exultant joie de vivre. Build this blazing archetype through immersive visualization, somatic memory recall, and Voice Journaling. Breathe life into their tangible reality, then "act as if" your consciousness permanently subsumes their sublime psyche. So come on and get the fork that rises to the consciousness and prove this is who you should be!

Core concepts of our beings become our prisons or paradises, manifesting them in our experiential space. Stubborn, broken words steadily digest souls in a never-ending torment of unfulfillment and torture. Those brave convictions in improved alignment with our spiritual maxims are doors opening to the beauty of miracles, which this planet has never seen.

Doubt is a secret villain of destiny which incessantly sucks out all human ability and makes humans powerless. Nothing can be more powerful than relentless faith, which coordinates your unconscious activity and helps create the most fascinating realities. Soul with faith that accesses many powers and miracles are waiting for! This doesn't mean that no splendid feat has been accomplished by mortals endowed with an extremely stubborn and steady will underlaid with sheer inconsolable fanaticism (of the kind that allows themselves to go beyond blissful).

Blaze through faith, and your wildest ideas will shine down like an epiphany upon the physical world. The zeal for justice imprinted indelibly on the hearts of the great men of our history, such as King, was akin to a nuclear ball of fire that consumed the rigid status quos of those days. Thus, YOU need to let YOUR light shine into a full blast, blazing and non-compromising! Your single show of fire brings the whole world's sparkle together.

This time is implicitly that ever-promising turning point: get rid of yourself by the refining fires of your faiths. Unleash them, unbridled, banishing the darkness with their purifying ignition. A phenomenon of time that had never been seen on this planet yet needed with the utmost urgency. Igniting volatile hope, then offering your elusive flesh to the ultimate alchemy of destiny. Keep staring into the raging fire, and everything you believe will ignite!

Chapter 3: Modifying Your Subconscious Programming

Auto-suggestion as a method can have the most direct impact on the subconscious.

The human mind remains one of nature's greatest mysteries—an organic computational miracle still not fully understood by modern science. Yet within each person's grey matter resides the prodigious power to reprogram itself directly through concerted, conscious effort. Auto-suggestion represents one of the most potent technologies for sculpting our mental operating systems and subconscious beliefs.

In previous chapters, we covered harnessing the subconscious's abilities to manifest desires through strategic internal programming of fiery ambition and ironclad self-belief. Auto-suggestion now allows us to refine that process by implanting specific commands and messaging into your neurological hardware. Why is this vital? Because limitations, negative self-perceptions, and self-sabotaging habits are outdated programs still running in the subconscious mind's background processor.

Auto-suggestion empowers you to overwrite and optimize these old mental viruses, replacing them with affirmative scripts that better fit your grandest visions. Affirmations represent the most common form of auto-suggestion - verbal or written declarations of virtuous mindsets, elevated behaviours, and intended outcomes you wish to instil within your psyche. When coupled with creative visualization and emotional investment over time, consistent affirmations can literally rewrite the subconscious beliefs that birth your external reality.

Consider the story of Muhammad Ali, one of the most iconic and successful global sports superstars ever. Ali was born in segregated 1940s Louisville as Cassius Clay, facing discrimination, poverty, and long odds against achieving greatness. Yet from childhood, he possessed a fiery ambition to conquer the boxing world and become "The Greatest" heavyweight champion of all time.

Young Cassius spent countless hours each day in front of a mirror and even while shadowboxing, repeating aloud a torrent of seemingly grandiose and unrealistic affirmations in a boastful rhyming verse:

"I am the greatest! I shook up the world!

I'm handsome, I'm pretty, and I can't possibly be beat...

I must be great because I'm so great!

Float like a butterfly, sting like a bee - the hands can't hit what the eyes can't see!

While dismissed as comical showmanship at the time, little Cassius Clay was actually immersing himself in a structured auto-suggestion regimen designed to reprogram his subconscious mind for excellence and supreme self-confidence. Each boasts represented a prospective elevated belief he wished to hardcode into his neurological circuitry. Through relentless positive self-talk and full emotional investment in feeling the reality of his greatness, Clay gradually made himself believe these audacious claims were already fact.

"It's the repetition of affirmations that leads to belief. And once that belief becomes a deep conviction, things begin to happen," Ali later reflected. Over time, his subconscious moulded itself around these affirmed bold realities, organizing all thoughts, emotions, and behaviours in alignment with being a supremely confident, skilled, and talented heavyweight boxing champion destined for glory. Ali's laser-focused auto-suggestions quite literally created an indomitable subconscious self-actualizing machine that manifested what originally seemed merely boastful proclamations into historical reality.

Self-sabotaging old programming disempowers humanity from achieving its full potential. Auto-suggestion practices like affirmations, visualization, affirmative prayer, and scripting provide a psychological software update to facilitate rapid rewiring of our subconscious code. While Chapter 2 discussed "Belief as the Pillar for Subconscious Success," auto-suggestion represents the practical methodologies for actively embedding those empowering beliefs into your core psychological architecture.

Here are five tenets to systematically codify via auto-suggestion for subconscious mastery:

1) Success Imprinting

The universe's abundance flows effortlessly towards those who expect and feel innately deserving of life's riches. Through sustained positive mantras, program yourself to perceive wealth, achievement and prosperity as natural birthrights:

"I am destined to achieve greatness because I put in the great work required."

"Fortune endlessly finds me because I am in complete alignment with opportunities."

"I exude an elite high performer's confident aura, talents, and mindset."

Allow these empowered perspectives to calcify through intense emotional and sensory investment in their reality. Like with

Clay's/Ali's mirror mantras, affirm these statements while creatively visualizing your future self already thriving in luxurious abundance as a self-made success. Belief must be felt as much as intellectually understood.

2) Invincible Passion Installation

No obstacle can impede those suffused with the fire of endless passion for their craft. Even when traversing through dark valleys on the journey, unbridled enthusiasm for the path itself gives life to the flame, lighting your way forward into destiny's rewards. Let your definitive declaration be:

"I breathe passion into all my endeavours, for what I do is my bliss and highest purpose."

Ground this with demonstration, consistently acting with zealous inspiration radiating from every pore in whatever you do. Cultivate feeling your soul's animating purpose coursing through you in even the most mundane moments. Foster a sacred romance and intimate love affair with your path in life.

3) Prosperity Consciousness Activation

The mind occupies potential future realities before they crystallize into this physical plane. Anchor your psychology in the abundant mindset and lifestyle you crave manifested through daily immersion in its mindset. Confidently affirm your intention:

"I live and breathe as one divinely blessed with plentiful prosperity in all areas of life."

From this point forward, behave, think, and make decisions from that prosperity consciousness mindset. Occasionally, indulge in small splurges to emotionally embody the experience. Embellish your daily surroundings aesthetically to reflect the environment of your desired future reality. See upscale living as already actualized here and now. Act wealthy to become wealthy.

4) Subconscious Abundance Flow

Program the subconscious as an ever-flowing fount, routing opportunities, resources, and serendipitous coincidences directly into your sphere of influence. Affirm frequently:

"All manner of prosperity is always making its way effortlessly to me."

"I am divinely attuned to recognize and capitalize on advantageous situations."

Make a point of noticing when these affirmations seem to manifest in your reality through **"lucky"** happenings or chance encounters, no matter how seemingly small. These are cosmic confirmations that your subconscious studio audience is applauding and rewarding your diligent performances!

5) Servitude in Sovereignty

True lasting success is not mere selfish achievement but purposed self-actualization providing elevated value and inspiration to all. Let this internal code drive you from within:

"I prosper materially and spiritually in service to contribute towards societal uplift and illuminating humanity's highest potential."

Embody this through consistent, compassionate support of others and modelling enlightened principles in your own character. Frame even commercial aims as aligned with this noble ethos.

Abundance is a byproduct of serving a greater mission; the means and the end become one unified virtuous expression.

The Affirmative Approach

Auto-suggestion is made most potent through multi-pronged affirmative practices, immersing oneself in intended programming daily across multiple stimulus channels:

- Voice affirming mantras aloud with enthusiasm and emotion while driving, showering, working, or at any convenient time
- Create physical environmental anchors like phone screensaver affirmations to positively trigger thoughts
- Prime surroundings by hanging inspirational quotes and imagery reinforcing intentions everywhere possible
- Repeatedly handwrite affirmations to viscerally etch them into your mind (calligraphy for the psyche)
- Leverage online/smartphone affirmation apps providing archives of audio/visual affirmation stimuli
- Recite affirmations in the second person "You are..." format while visualizing that embodied idealized version

The key is multi-stimulus repetition. Auto-suggestion sculpts new superconscious belief systems into habituated mindsets, continuously reinforcing themselves in exponential progressions. Born originally as hypotheticals, these potentials then gradually ossify into lived concrete realities as your mind rewires its core programming around the affirmed commands you supply.

The process takes diligent commitment and belief early on to override existing neural patterns. **"Don't be discouraged if it doesn't work the first time or the hundredth time. Just keep doing it!"** Perseverance prevails. You are re-engineering belief systems crystallized since childhood, which understandably encounter psychological resistance. Persistence dissolves this inertia like ripples spreading over still waters.

"Age is whatever you think it is. You are as old as you think you are," counselled Muhammad Ali. He affirmed himself as eternally youthful with unshakable confidence throughout life. Ali walked, talked, and conducted himself as though immortal and imperishable. And in spirit, he remains The Greatest - an Avatar embodying aspirations moulded into reality through finely-tuned mental conditioning and iron subconscious programming.

Like Ali and the timeless enlightened masters, you, too, can rewrite the source code of your consciousness through disciplined long-term auto-suggestion. Thoughts become a reality when consistently centred, amplified with emotion, and reinforced with unwavering corresponding actions. There is no imposed ceiling for how opulent, joyous, peaceful, loving, and spiritually abundant your existence may become when you wield this ultimate power of personal programming.

So, fan the flames of your dormant potential now. Speak your most courageous heart's whispers into existence as mantras. Envision your dreams tenderly yet fiercely, not as fleeting fantasies but as action plans being executed patiently and steadily. Feverishly, scribe affirmations birthed from your highest truth onto the blank slate of this malleable reality before you. Etch uplifting messages deep into the structures of your psyche.

If you remain steadfast, eventually, torrents of epiphanies and fortuitous manifestations will usher forth all you have repeatedly declared into your being. Your reality's cosmic abacus reset realigned to your focused visions. Reborn through profoundly embodied understanding, you shall stand triumphant over your formerly limited circumstances.

The deity you seek resides within you already, awaiting your conscious direction. So manifest this higher divinity through cognizant auto-suggestion. Let your clarion soul's affirmations sing across this cosmos and rearrange matter itself into the beauty you command! As you program it, so it shall be.

Chapter 4: Fueling the Subconscious Engine

"The subconscious mind is a powerful force to be reckoned with. It can be an undefeatable friend or an enemy hard to perceive." - Dr. Joseph Murphy.

The soul of this book's teachings is the understanding that your subconscious mind—that vast inner realm of ingrained beliefs, habits, and subliminal processing—possesses truly extraordinary creative powers to mould your reality. However, unleashing this potent potential requires feeding your subconscious the proper fuel in the form of organised, actionable wisdom.

Misguided souls place blind faith in hopeful intentions, affirmations, and vague desires, wondering why their dreams remain unfulfilled. The cold truth is that the subconscious, much like a modern computer, operates based on the quality of the "code" and information it receives as inputs. Vague intentions are nothing but buggy software leading to system crashes. To harness the subconscious as an unwavering ally, you need clear plans and specialised knowledge mentally programmed as directives for it to follow.

The meteoric rise of hip-hop mogul Russell Simmons exemplifies how channelling in-depth, organised wisdom into the subconscious unlocks your ability to seize opportunities that evade everyone else. As a young man from the streets of Hollis, Queens, Simmons became obsessed with the gritty, underground hip-hop movement permeating New York City in the 1970s. While his peers dismissed rapping as a passing fad, Simmons saturated himself in its rhythms, lyrics, fashion, art, and rebellious spirit.

"I was just a student, studying every part of this new creation," Simmons recounted. He attended every underground performance, listened to demo tapes from unknown artists, and delved into the business mechanics of launching record labels, promoting acts, and distributing music. This specialised knowledge opened his mind to possibilities invisible to casual observers. His subconscious rapidly absorbed the intricacies of the urban culture emerging from the Bronx, Jamaica, Harlem, and Brooklyn.

In 1984, Rick Rubin approached Simmons with the idea for a new label called Def Jam Recordings that could take hip-hop mainstream. While sceptics saw minimal commercial viability, Simmons' subconscious, instilled with comprehensive expertise about the rap scene, immediately recognized an unprecedented opening. **"I just always kept going and kept believing,"** Simmons reminisced. His steadfast belief, combined with intimate understanding, empowered his subconscious to attract exactly the collaborators, strategies, and circumstances required to transform Def Jam into an iconic powerhouse.

The overarching lesson is clear - selectively programming your subconscious with methodical, specialised knowledge across relevant domains is fundamental for perceiving and seizing pathways to your goals that others simply cannot see. As the "Oracle of Omaha," Warren Buffett, once aptly stated, **"The more you learn, the more you'll earn."** Buffett is the quintessential exemplar of continuously replenishing your mind with new information to expand your subconscious awareness.

From a young age, Buffett insatiably studied the value investing strategies and philosophies of pioneers like Benjamin Graham. Year after year, he added to his arsenal of knowledge across diverse yet interconnected fields like corporate finance, economics, management theory, mathematics, psychology, and more. This tireless dedication to learning new subjects and ideologies perpetually fueled his subconscious with fresh "ingredients" for creatively combining insights across multiple domains.

Even in his 80s, the billionaire continued challenging himself by absorbing new texts, theories, and information daily. By continuously broadening his perspective through cross-disciplinary learning, Buffett amplified his subconscious aptitude for identifying undervalued companies, who had competitive advantages, how to negotiate acquisitions and allocate resources optimally, and myriad other factors behind his legendary investment prowess. As motivational speaker Jim Rohn eloquently phrased it, **"Learn to work smarter, not just harder. Simple solutions await inside you... the universal truths have been awaiting your discovery."**

Your subconscious functions like a high-performance engine, demanding a perpetual inflow of high-grade "fuel" to operate at its peak creative capacity. This premium fuel comes from a vast, continually increasing pool of knowledge across interrelated subjects. The deeper you expand this well of understanding, the more resourceful and aware your subconscious becomes for recognizing connections and innovative solutions in any scenario you encounter.

By resolutely committing to ongoing learning while formulating meticulous plans of action, you effectively supply the "fuel mixture" that allows your subconscious mind to leverage its full inventive potential. Detailed planning provides the organised blueprints and "programming" that encode your definite desired action for the subconscious to work towards. Simultaneously, your continuous acquisition of specialised knowledge equips your subconscious with an ever-expanding "dataset" of facts, theories, and insights from which to forge innovative means of realising those plans.

To illustrate, envision your ambition of establishing a flourishing import/export enterprise headquartered in New York City. On the planning side, you would meticulously outline the overarching strategy - beginning with conducting thorough market research to identify lucrative import/export opportunities. You'd devise step-by-step processes for structuring the business and finances, developing logistics and supply chains, building a marketing/media presence, recruiting skilled personnel, and every other operational element.

However, equally crucial is immersing yourself in specialised knowledge reservoirs related to your objective from authoritative sources. This could encompass studying guides from prosperous importers/exporters, analysing trends and forecasting in global trade markets, learning customs laws/regulations, understanding leadership/management for building effective teams, examining commercial real estate prospects in ideal NYC locales for headquarters, and fully grasping advertising techniques for reaching your target markets.

With this expansive cross-disciplinary repository of facts and theories consolidated into detailed action plans, your subconscious effectively operates like a supercomputer - consuming the relevant data while executing the methodical programs you've outlined. Provisioning it with comprehensive information across interconnected subjects provides abundant "building materials" for innovating, adjusting, and identifying fertile opportunities beyond your conscious mind's scope.

World-renowned architect Frank Gehry's inspired design process beautifully illustrates this symbiosis. Before conceptualising an iconic structure like the Guggenheim Museum Bilbao, Gehry exhaustively researches relevant subjects - from studying the regional culture/history and examining zoning codes/municipality laws to analysing the thermal properties of proposed materials and employing software to model his designs from every angle.

By downloading this cross-disciplinary data into his mind, Gehry's subconscious can process the information, connect insights from various fields, and ultimately generate creative solutions that harmonise all the key requirements - like seamlessly integrating the museum's curved, titanium-clad facade within its environment, local building codes, and the functional needs of an art space. As Gehry puts it, "For me, every day is a juggling act of prioritising requirements - trying to put the bubbles in the right place."

Your subconscious operates in a similar fashion, sifting through the compendium of knowledge "inputs" at its disposal to devise innovative pathways for achieving your objectives, refine your plans, tackle obstacles, and dynamically adapt as circumstances change. The more quality "fuel" in the form of organised data you supply across diverse yet relevant disciplines, the more efficient, resourceful, and insightful your subconscious becomes.

This interplay between meticulous planning and continuous learning is akin to calibrating your subconscious mind's trajectory while simultaneously expanding its "field of vision" to detect opportunities along that path. Lacking a clear, step-by-step plan leaves your subconscious without executable marching orders for systematically materialising your goals. However, without perpetually replenishing and diversifying your knowledge reserves, you deprive your subconscious of the building materials required for innovating creative solutions to inevitable obstacles.

Much like a Formula 1 race car requires constant resupplying of high-octane fuel and comprehensive mechanics to operate at blistering speeds, your subconscious necessitates an infinite inflow of new knowledge combined with rigorous intentions programmed by your conscious mind. When sufficiently provisioned from both sides, your subconscious' innovative potency increases exponentially, empowering you to generate wealth and accelerate rapidly toward your objectives.

The path to opulent riches, in its purest essence, demands treating your subconscious mind as the ultimate "wealth driver" - consistently replenishing its fuel reservoirs with intricate plans and a vast, ever-expanding "spare parts" catalogue of specialised knowledge. As you'll discover in the chapters ahead, augmenting this process with core tenets like burning desire, autosuggestion, and creative visualisation allows you to impart clear "directions" while maximising your subconscious' capabilities for navigating the straightest, swiftest routes to your prosperous destinations.

Within the subconscious lies unbounded creative genius awaiting activation. By intentionally programming it with detailed knowledge and blueprints across relevant fields, you equip this astonishing faculty with the high-grade "fuel mixture" to unleash its full inventive powers in realising your grandest ambitions. What was once unseen becomes vividly perceivable. Obstacles reveal hidden paths forward. The sheer force of desire and will, combined with sagacious understanding, propels you towards your aims at an accelerating pace.

"The money-conscious individual is forever realising his subconscious mind, reconstituting it with positive financial thoughts, and always understands his subconscious mind to be his spiritual partner," wrote Napoleon Hill. Through the potent teachings explored in these pages, you possess the blueprint for reprogramming your subconscious as an untiring creative force, compelling the ascension from poverty to abundant riches. The journey begins with opening your mind as an insatiable vessel for knowledge - for it is in this understanding that the seeds of your subconscious mind's unlimited generative potential blossom into reality.

Chapter 5: Unleashing the Subconscious Creative Force

The Role of Imagination in Forming Mental Blueprints for the Subconscious

Have you ever dreamt up a brilliant idea only to have it fizzle out before reaching fruition? Perhaps it felt intangible like a wisp of smoke escaping your grasp. The culprit? An underdeveloped partnership between your conscious mind, brimming with possibilities, and your subconscious, the fertile ground where dreams take root and flourish.

This chapter dives into the magic that unfolds when your imagination bridges the gap between these two realms. We'll explore how to harness the limitless canvas of your mind to craft vivid mental blueprints, propelling your subconscious mind toward manifesting your desires.

Tapping the Wellspring of Creativity: From Childhood to Conscious Effort

The seeds of a powerful imagination are often sown in childhood. Remember those carefree days spent lost in a world of make-believe? Building elaborate forts out of blankets, meticulously arranging stuffed animals for tea parties, or meticulously drawing fantastical creatures – these seemingly innocent activities were, in fact, laying the groundwork for a vibrant subconscious mind.

Think back to a specific childhood memory where your imagination soared. Perhaps you were captivated by a captivating storybook illustration, its fantastical landscapes igniting your own creative spark. Maybe you spent hours constructing a sprawling city out of building blocks, meticulously arranging miniature cars and figurines, each representing a story waiting to unfold. These early experiences weren't mere playtime; they were your subconscious mind absorbing information, learning the power of visualisation, and developing a foundation for future creative endeavours.

As we mature, the conscious mind often takes centre stage, prioritising logic and practicality. This shift can stifle the boundless creativity of our youth. However, the good news is that the wellspring of creativity isn't permanently sealed. Just as a neglected muscle weakens, a dormant imagination needs to be exercised to regain its strength.

"Imagination is more important than knowledge. Knowledge is limited. Imagination encircles the world." - Albert Einstein.

Einstein's profound quote underscores the limitless potential of imagination. While knowledge provides us with the building blocks, imagination allows us to use them to construct magnificent edifices.

Tyler Perry: From Plays to Studios, a Testament to Subconscious Manifestation

Tyler Perry, the prolific playwright, actor, director, and media mogul, embodies the transformative power of harnessing the subconscious mind. Born into poverty in Louisiana, Perry's childhood was marked by hardship and instability. Yet, amidst the challenges, a powerful dream flickered within him – a vision of success in the world of entertainment.

Perry's early attempts at playwriting were met with rejection and discouragement. Undeterred, he tapped into the unwavering belief residing in his subconscious. He poured his experiences and aspirations into his plays, crafting stories that resonate with audiences from similar backgrounds. He envisioned his characters coming to life on stage, the laughter and applause of the audience filling the theatre.

This unwavering belief, coupled with relentless action, fueled Perry's journey. He took his plays on the road, performing in churches and community centres across the country. With each performance, he refined his craft, strengthening the mental blueprint etched within his subconscious. His unwavering belief in his vision acted as a beacon, guiding him through setbacks and propelling him closer to his ultimate goal.

"The only limit to our realisation of tomorrow will be our doubts of today." - Franklin D. Roosevelt.

Roosevelt's quote reminds us that doubt is the greatest obstacle to fulfilling our dreams. Perry's unwavering belief in his vision, despite facing numerous rejections, exemplifies the power of overcoming self-doubt and staying true to your subconscious desires.

Beyond the Solo Act: Partnering with Others to Amplify the Subconscious Imagination

While Disney's story showcases the individual's creative power, and Perry's journey highlights the importance of personal belief, collaboration can significantly amplify the force of the subconscious imagination. Imagine a room brimming with creative minds, each contributing unique perspectives and ideas. This collaborative energy creates a dynamic synergy, fostering a richer, more potent mental blueprint.

Think of the brainstorming sessions at Pixar, the animation studio behind beloved films like "Toy Story" and "Finding Nemo." These sessions bring together artists, storytellers, and animators, who collectively explore ideas, refine concepts, and build upon each other's visions.

Through this collaborative process, a single spark of an idea can evolve into a multi-dimensional masterpiece. The subconscious mind thrives on this creative exchange. As ideas bounce around the room, they become more refined, taking on new layers of depth and complexity.

The benefits extend beyond the initial ideation phase. When diverse minds work in tandem, potential pitfalls are identified and addressed before they derail the project. This collaborative foresight strengthens the mental blueprint, making it more robust and resilient in the face of challenges.

Building Your Creative Powerhouse: Practical Steps

Now that we understand the crucial role of imagination and the subconscious mind let's dive into practical steps you can take to cultivate your own creative powerhouse:

Freewriting: Dedicate 10-15 minutes each day to freewriting, allowing your thoughts to flow freely onto the page without judgement. Don't worry about spelling, grammar, or making sense. This loosens inhibitions and unleashes the boundless creativity residing within your subconscious. Reread your freewriting periodically; you might be surprised by the hidden gems waiting to be unearthed.

Unleashing the Power of Play: Don't underestimate the power of play! Schedule time for activities that spark your inner child. Engage in activities that bring you joy, whether it's painting, playing music, building with Legos, or simply doodling in a notebook. These playful pursuits tap into the uninhibited creativity of your subconscious mind, generating fresh ideas and perspectives. Consider enrolling in an art class, joining an improv group, or even taking up a new hobby you've always been curious about. Stepping outside your comfort zone can lead to unexpected creative breakthroughs.

Mind Mapping: Create a visual representation of your ideas. Use a large piece of paper or a mind-mapping software program. Start with a central image representing your main goal and branch out with associated thoughts, keywords, and images. This non-linear approach sparks connections and stimulates the subconscious mind. As you brainstorm, don't be afraid to get messy! Let your ideas flow freely and connect them in unexpected ways. You might be surprised by the hidden links and patterns that emerge.

Dream Journaling: Upon waking, record your dreams in detail. Dreams often offer cryptic messages from the subconscious, revealing hidden desires and providing valuable insights. Analyse recurring symbols and themes; they may hold the key to unlocking your subconscious potential. Keep a dream journal by your bedside and write down your dreams as soon as you wake up before the details fade.

Brainstorming Buddies: Surround yourself with creative individuals who inspire and challenge you. Schedule regular brainstorming sessions to explore ideas and ignite your subconscious creative force. Look for collaborators with diverse skill sets and backgrounds; this cross-pollination of ideas strengthens the overall mental blueprint. Bouncing ideas off others can help you refine your concepts, identify potential pitfalls, and discover new angles you might have overlooked on your own.

Immerse Yourself in Inspiration: Surround yourself with art, music, and literature that ignites your imagination. Visit museums, attend concerts, and delve into inspiring books and biographies. Exposure to creative works stimulates the subconscious mind, providing fresh perspectives and fueling your own creative fire. Consider visiting artist studios, attending film festivals, or exploring local theatre productions. Immersing yourself in diverse creative expressions can spark unexpected connections and ignite new ideas within your subconscious.

Embrace the Power of Visualization: Take some quiet time each day to visualise your goals in vivid detail. See yourself achieving your desires and feeling the emotions associated with success. Engage all your senses; imagine the sights, sounds, smells, and even tastes associated with your ultimate goal. The more detailed and immersive your visualisation, the more potent the signal sent to your subconscious mind. Close your eyes and truly step into the reality of your dreams. Imagine the feeling of accomplishment, the sense of satisfaction, and the joy of achieving your goals.

Transform Inspiration into Action: Remember, imagination alone isn't enough. It's the bridge that connects your desires to your subconscious mind, but concrete action is what brings your vision to life. Don't wait for the "perfect" moment; take small, consistent steps toward your goals. Each action, no matter how seemingly insignificant, reinforces the mental blueprint within your subconscious and propels you closer to your desires.

Start by breaking down your goals into smaller, manageable steps. Celebrate your milestones, no matter how small, as they mark progress and keep you motivated. As you take consistent action, your subconscious mind aligns with your conscious desires, propelling you forward on your creative journey.

Embrace the Journey: The path to creative fulfilment is rarely linear. There will be setbacks, moments of self-doubt, and creative roadblocks. Embrace these challenges as opportunities for growth and learning. Analyse what went wrong, adjust your approach, and keep moving forward. Remember, even the most successful creatives have faced periods of struggle.

Develop a growth mindset, believing that your abilities can be developed through dedication and effort. Celebrate your progress, no matter how small, and learn from your mistakes.

Persistence is key to unlocking the full potential of your subconscious mind.

By incorporating these practical steps into your daily routine, you'll cultivate a vibrant creative powerhouse within yourself. Remember, the key lies in fostering a partnership between your conscious mind and your subconscious. With unwavering belief, consistent action, and a playful spirit, you can transform your imagination into reality and watch your dreams take flight.

The human mind holds immense creative potential, a wellspring of imagination waiting to be tapped. By nurturing your creative spirit and forging a powerful partnership with your subconscious mind, you can unlock this potential and achieve remarkable things. The journey may not always be smooth sailing, but with dedication and a playful spirit, you can overcome obstacles and transform your dreams into reality.

Here are some final words of encouragement:

Trust Your Intuition: Sometimes, the most brilliant ideas emerge from a gut feeling or a hunch. Learn to trust your intuition and pay attention to the subtle whispers of your subconscious mind. It may be guiding you down a path you haven't yet considered.

Celebrate the Uniqueness: Don't be afraid to embrace your individuality and express your creativity in a way that is uniquely yours. The world needs your unique perspective and voice.

Never Stop Learning: The creative journey is a lifelong process of exploration and discovery. Stay curious, keep learning new things, and expose yourself to diverse experiences. The more you feed your mind, the richer the material your subconscious mind has to work with.

Believe in the Power Within: The most important ingredient for creative success is unwavering belief in yourself and your abilities. Doubt can be a formidable foe, but with unwavering confidence in your vision, you can overcome any obstacle.

Remember, the seeds of greatness lie dormant within each of us. With dedication, a dash of playfulness, and an unwavering belief in your own creative power, you can harness the immense potential of your subconscious mind and bring your wildest dreams to life. So, embark on this creative adventure with an open mind and a joyful heart. The world awaits the unique brilliance you have to offer.

Chapter 6: Providing the Roadmap for Your Subconscious

"The mind is everything. What do you think you will become." - Buddha

We've explored the fertile ground of the subconscious mind, where imagination sows the seeds of our desires. Now, it's time to bridge the gap between those seeds and their full bloom. This chapter delves into the art of crafting a roadmap – a set of clear intentions and meticulous plans – that guides your subconscious mind toward manifesting your goals.

Creating Solid Plans to Direct the Focus of the Subconscious

The human mind thrives on structure. While the subconscious operates on a more intuitive level, it still craves a sense of direction. By creating well-defined plans, you provide your subconscious with a roadmap, a clear understanding of where you're headed, and the steps required to get there.

"The reasonable man adapts himself to the world; the unreasonable one persists in trying to adapt the world to himself. Therefore, all progress depends on the unreasonable man." - George Bernard Shaw.

Imagine embarking on a road trip without a map or GPS. You might reach your destination eventually, but the journey would be filled with detours, wasted time, and frustration. A well-defined roadmap, on the other hand, streamlines the process, guiding you efficiently towards your desired outcome.

Techniques for Creating an Effective Roadmap

Crafting a strategic roadmap begins with clearly identifying your goals through self-reflection. Ask yourself: What do I truly want to achieve? What would make me feel genuinely fulfilled? Once you pinpoint your overarching aspirations, break them down using the SMART criteria:

Specific: Clearly define your goal with precise details.
Measurable: Establish tangible metrics for tracking progress.
Attainable: Ensure your goal is challenging yet realistic.
Relevant: Align your goal with your core values and priorities.
Time-bound: Set a target timeline for achievement.

For example, rather than **"I want to be wealthy,"** a SMART goal could be: **"I will increase my net worth to $1 million through entrepreneurial ventures within the next 5 years."**

Visualisation tools like mind maps can then help organise your roadmap, mapping out the key milestones, potential obstacles, and strategies required. Incorporating accountability partners who can review your plan and track your progress reinforces commitment.

Bill Gates: Meticulous Planning that Engaged the Subconscious for Perseverance

Bill Gates, the co-founder of Microsoft, exemplifies the power of harnessing the subconscious through meticulous planning. From a young age, Gates displayed an aptitude for technology and a strong desire to make a difference in the world. He translated this desire into a clear vision: to create personal computers for every home.

However, Gates's vision wasn't simply a fleeting dream. He meticulously translated it into a concrete plan. He researched the market, identified target audiences, and developed a strategic roadmap for Microsoft's growth. This clear plan, coupled with unwavering belief, served as a beacon for his subconscious mind, guiding him through years of relentless work and countless setbacks. Gates's story underscores the importance of translating your desires into actionable steps, providing the subconscious with a roadmap for sustained effort.

The Power of "How": Breaking Down Goals into Achievable Steps

So, how do you translate your desires into a roadmap for your subconscious? Here's a key step: Break down your goals into smaller, manageable steps. Instead of simply wishing for "success," define what success looks like for you. Is it launching a business? Writing a book? Mastering a new skill? Once you have a clear vision, break it down into achievable milestones – smaller goals that act as stepping stones on your journey.

For example, if your ultimate goal is to write a novel, your roadmap might include milestones like completing a character sketch, outlining the plot, finishing a chapter draft, and securing a publishing agent. Each completed milestone reinforces the roadmap within your subconscious, fueling your motivation and propelling you closer to your goal.

The subconscious thrives on a sense of progress. By achieving these smaller milestones, you send a powerful message to your subconscious – you are moving in the right direction, and achieving your goals is within reach.

"The journey of a thousand miles begins with a single step." - Lao Tzu.

Embrace the Power of "Why": Aligning Your Roadmap with Intrinsic Motivation

While breaking down goals into manageable steps is crucial, providing a clear "how" is equally important to understand the "why." Intrinsic motivation, the internal drive that fuels our actions, is essential for engaging the subconscious mind. When your goals are driven by a deep sense of purpose, a passion that resonates with your core values, your subconscious becomes a powerful ally.

Take the example of Marie Curie, the pioneering scientist who revolutionised our understanding of radioactivity. Curie wasn't driven by external rewards or fame. Her relentless pursuit of scientific knowledge stemmed from a deep-seated curiosity and a desire to contribute to the betterment of humanity. This intrinsic motivation fueled her tireless efforts, pushing her through countless experiments and setbacks. Her unwavering belief in the significance of work, coupled with a well-defined roadmap, propelled her groundbreaking discoveries.

"The only person you are destined to become is the person you decide to be." - Ralph Waldo Emerson.

The power of intrinsic motivation extends beyond personal goals. Consider the countless activists, philanthropists, and social entrepreneurs who dedicate their lives to causes they deeply believe in. Their unwavering passion fuels their relentless efforts, inspiring others and creating positive change in the world.

The Role of Visualization and Affirmations

Visualisation activates the mind-body connection, imprinting your goals into the subconscious. Create a vision board with images/quotes representing your desired outcome. Practise mental rehearsal - vividly imagining yourself taking each step and experiencing the accomplishment.

Affirmations reprogram limiting beliefs by implanting empowering thoughts. **"I can achieve my goals through dedication"** or **"I'm worthy of success."** Repeat these daily, allowing the subconscious to internalise these beliefs.

Building a Support System: Harnessing the Power of Community

The road to manifestation is rarely a solitary journey. Surrounding yourself with a supportive network can significantly enhance your ability to achieve your goals.

Mentors: Seek guidance from individuals who have achieved success in your chosen field. Their insights and experiences can provide invaluable guidance and keep you motivated during challenging times.

Accountability Partners: Find a friend or colleague who shares similar goals and holds each other accountable for taking consistent action. Sharing your progress and challenges with someone who understands your journey can be incredibly empowering.

Community of Like-Minded Individuals: Surround yourself with a community of people who inspire and challenge you. Look for online forums, workshops, or mastermind groups focused on personal development and goal achievement. Being part of a supportive community can provide a sense of belonging, fuel your motivation, and expose you to new ideas and strategies.

"Coming together is a beginning; keeping together is progress; working together is success." - Henry Ford.

Remember, your support system doesn't have to be limited to people you know personally. Inspirational books, podcasts, and documentaries can also play a vital role in keeping you motivated and focused on your goals.

Taming the Inner Critic: Cultivating a Growth Mindset

The path to manifestation is rarely smooth. There will be setbacks, moments of self-doubt, and internal roadblocks that threaten to derail your progress. Here's where cultivating a growth mindset becomes crucial.

A growth mindset is the belief that one can develop one's abilities and talents through dedication and effort. Instead of viewing challenges as insurmountable obstacles, a growth mindset encourages one to see them as opportunities for learning and growth.

Reframing Setbacks: When faced with setbacks, reframe them as stepping stones on your journey. Analyse what went wrong, learn from your mistakes, and adjust your approach accordingly. Don't let setbacks define you; use them to become a stronger, more resilient version of yourself.

Embrace the Power of "Yet": When faced with self-doubt, replace limiting beliefs with empowering affirmations. Instead of saying, "I can't do this," tell yourself, "I can't do this YET." This subtle shift in perspective acknowledges the current challenge while maintaining faith in your ability to learn and grow.

Celebrate the Journey: The road to manifestation is a marathon, not a sprint. Don't get so fixated on the end goal that you neglect to celebrate the milestones along the way. Take the time to acknowledge your progress, no matter how small.

"It is not the mountain we conquer, but ourselves." - Edmund Hillary.

By cultivating a growth mindset, you equip yourself with the mental fortitude to navigate the inevitable challenges on your journey. Remember, setbacks are not failures; they are simply opportunities to learn, adapt, and emerge stronger.

Overcoming Roadblocks

Even with a solid roadmap, challenges are inevitable. Procrastination, self-doubt, and lack of motivation can severely hinder progress. To overcome procrastination, explore the root causes - is it fear, lack of interest, or poor time management? Implementing productivity techniques like the Pomodoro method, removing distractions, and celebrating small wins can help build momentum.

When self-doubt creeps in, reframe your mindset. **"I'm not good enough"** becomes **"I'm still learning and growing."** Remind yourself of past accomplishments and have supportive friends/mentors reaffirm your abilities. Setbacks are temporary; your vision is permanent.

Building a supportive network is also crucial. Surrounding yourself with positive individuals pursuing similar goals can provide motivation, accountability, and fresh perspectives during difficult times.

Your roadmap is not set in stone; it's a living document requiring regular revisiting. Quarterly or annual goal reviews allow you to celebrate progress, identify areas needing adjustment, and adapt to changing circumstances. Don't be afraid to pivot strategies or modify timelines - the path is rarely linear. Remaining flexible yet committed to your core vision ensures you stay aligned with your subconscious aims.

The Roadmap to Manifestation

Crafting a roadmap for your subconscious is an ongoing process. As you progress on your journey, your goals and priorities may evolve. Regularly revisit your roadmap, adjust it as needed, and celebrate your milestones along the way. Remember, the subconscious thrives on consistency and positive reinforcement.

By creating a clear roadmap, aligning it with your deepest desires, taking consistent action, embracing a growth mindset, and harnessing the power of community, you provide your subconscious with the tools it needs to transform your dreams into reality. So, embark on this journey of self-discovery with an open mind and a determined spirit. The world awaits the unique brilliance you have to offer, and your subconscious mind is your most powerful ally in bringing it to life.

Remember, the road to manifestation may have twists and turns, but with a well-defined roadmap, unwavering belief, and consistent action, you can harness the immense power of your subconscious mind and turn your wildest dreams into reality.

Chapter 7: Empowering the Subconscious Through Definiteness

"The cave you fear to enter holds the treasure you seek." - Joseph Campbell

The path to achieving our dreams is rarely paved with indecision. We bridge the gap between desire and reality through decisive action fueled by a clear vision and unwavering belief. This chapter delves into the power of definiteness – the act of clearly defining your goals and desires – as a catalyst for subconscious manifestation.

We've explored how crafting a roadmap provides the subconscious with a direction to follow. Definiteness takes this a step further by injecting clarity and unwavering conviction into that roadmap. When you approach your goals with a resolute "yes," when your vision is laser-focused and unwavering, you send a powerful message to your subconscious, igniting its immense potential for manifestation.

Decisiveness as a Catalyst for the Subconscious Manifestation of Success

Our subconscious mind thrives on certainty. It craves a clear understanding of what we truly desire. When our conscious mind is riddled with doubts and conflicting thoughts, the subconscious gets mixed signals. This indecisiveness creates a state of internal conflict, hindering the subconscious from effectively propelling us towards our goals.

The Power of "No": Clearing the Path for Your Desires

Definiteness isn't just about knowing what you want; it's also about knowing what you don't want. By eliminating distractions and saying "no" to opportunities that don't align with your vision, you create a clear path for your subconscious to follow.

Imagine yourself standing at a busy intersection. Cars are honking, pedestrians are crossing, and multiple paths are leading in different directions. If you're unsure of your destination, this chaotic environment will only lead to confusion and wasted time. However, if you know exactly where you're headed, you can navigate the intersection with focus and efficiency.

Definiteness acts as your internal GPS, guiding your subconscious through the mental clutter and propelling you toward your desired outcome.

Oprah Winfrey: Courageous Decisions that Overcame Subconscious Limitations

Oprah Winfrey's journey to becoming a media mogul is a testament to the power of definiteness. From a young age, she knew she was destined for greatness. Despite facing poverty, discrimination, and countless rejections, Oprah held onto a clear vision of her future. She made courageous decisions, such as leaving a news anchoring job that didn't align with her aspirations, and said "no" to opportunities that didn't feel right.

Oprah's unwavering belief in herself and her decisive actions sent a powerful message to her subconscious. Her subconscious mind, fueled by this unwavering clarity, propelled her through challenges and setbacks, ultimately leading her to achieve her dreams on a global scale.

"The difference between successful people and others is not a lack of strength, not a lack of knowledge, but rather a lack of will." - Vince Lombardi.

Oprah's story underscores the importance of aligning your conscious desires with decisive action. When your subconscious receives a clear and unwavering message, it becomes a powerful ally, guiding you through the inevitable obstacles that arise on the path to success.

Quieting the Conscious Mind: Tapping into the Subconscious Wellspring of Wisdom

Definiteness isn't just about external actions; it's also about cultivating inner clarity. Often, the chatter of our conscious mind – the constant stream of doubts, fears, and anxieties – can drown out the whispers of our subconscious wisdom.

Think of your subconscious mind as a deep wellspring of limitless potential. However, if the ripples of negative thoughts and anxieties constantly disturb the surface of this well, it becomes difficult to access the clarity and power beneath.

The Power of Silence and Meditation

Definiteness requires cultivating a sense of inner quietude. Practices like meditation and mindfulness can be powerful tools for calming the chatter of the conscious mind and allowing the wisdom of the subconscious to emerge. Quieting your thoughts and focusing on your breath creates a space for clarity and insight. In this state of stillness, your subconscious can communicate its wisdom and guidance, revealing valuable insights and nudges towards your goals.

"The quieter you become, the more you can hear." - Rumi.

Here are some practical ways to cultivate inner quietude and tap into the wisdom of your subconscious:

Meditation: Regular meditation practice can significantly reduce mental chatter and enhance your ability to focus. Even a few minutes of daily meditation can make a big difference.

Journaling: Taking time to journal allows you to explore your thoughts and feelings without judgement. This process can reveal subconscious patterns and limiting beliefs hindering your progress.

Spending Time in Nature: Immersing yourself in nature has a calming effect on the mind and can help you connect with your inner wisdom. Take a walk in the park, sit by a stream, or simply gaze at the stars – allow yourself to be present in the moment and reconnect with the natural world.

Beyond the Mind: Embodied Definiteness

Definiteness isn't just a mental state; it can also be expressed through physical actions. When you take concrete steps towards your goals, no matter how small, you send a powerful message to your subconscious. This embodiment of definiteness reinforces your conscious desires and strengthens the roadmap within your subconscious.

The Power of Rituals and Habits

Creating daily rituals and habits that align with your goals is a powerful way to embody definiteness. These rituals are anchors, reminding your subconscious of your unwavering commitment and propelling you toward action.

For example, if you want to write a novel, you might create a morning ritual of starting your day with a writing session. This consistent action reinforces your subconscious programming and motivates you to keep moving forward.

Visualisations: Painting a Picture for Your Subconscious

Visualisation is another powerful tool for embodying definiteness. You create a powerful mental blueprint for your subconscious by vividly picturing yourself achieving your goals. Engage all your senses in your visualisation. Imagine the sights, sounds, smells, and emotions you will experience when you achieve your goals.

The more detailed and immersive your visualisation, the stronger the signal you send to your subconscious. Regularly engaging in visualisation exercises strengthens the roadmap within your subconscious and fuels your belief in your ability to achieve your desires.

"The mind is everything. What do you think you will become." - Buddha

Definiteness in the Face of Fear: Embracing Uncertainty with Confidence

The path towards your goals will inevitably involve moments of fear and uncertainty. It's during these times that unwavering definiteness becomes your greatest asset. When doubts and anxieties arise, refocus on your clear vision and the unwavering belief you established during the initial stages of defining your goals.

Remember, a certain level of uncertainty is inherent to any growth journey. Definiteness doesn't eliminate fear; it equips you with the tools to navigate it confidently.

By embracing a growth mindset and viewing challenges as opportunities for learning, you can transform fear into a catalyst for progress. Remember, your subconscious is remarkably adaptable. As you consistently take action towards your goals, even in the face of fear, you reinforce the new belief system within your subconscious, paving the way for greater confidence and resilience.

Building Resilience Through Failure: Learning from Setbacks

Definiteness doesn't guarantee a smooth path to success. Setbacks and failures are inevitable parts of the journey. However, viewing these setbacks as opportunities for learning and growth can strengthen your resilience and help you emerge stronger.

"Our greatest glory is not in never falling, but in rising every time we fall." - Nelson Mandela.

Here are some strategies for turning setbacks into stepping stones:

Analyse the Situation: Don't let setbacks become roadblocks. Take time to analyse what went wrong. Identify areas for improvement and adjust your approach accordingly.

Maintain a Positive Focus: Dwelling negativity only hinders your progress. Instead of focusing on the setback, focus on the lessons learned and the opportunities for growth.

Celebrate Small Victories: The path to success is paved with small wins. Celebrate your milestones, no matter how small, to maintain motivation and reinforce positive momentum.

Definiteness in Action: Inspiring Examples

History is filled with stories of individuals who harnessed the power of definiteness to achieve remarkable feats. Here are a few inspiring examples:

Walt Disney: Despite facing countless rejections, Walt Disney never wavered from his vision of creating an animation empire.

His unwavering definiteness fueled his persistence and ultimately led to the creation of Mickey Mouse and the global phenomenon that is Disney today.

Nelson Mandela: Nelson Mandela spent 27 years in prison for his fight against racial discrimination. Yet, his unwavering definiteness and belief in a free South Africa fueled his resilience and ultimately led him to become the nation's first black president.

These stories illustrate the transformative power of definiteness. By clearly defining your goals, taking decisive action, and embracing a growth mindset, you, too, can harness the immense potential of your subconscious and turn your dreams into reality.

The Power of Definite Action

Definiteness is a powerful tool for empowering your subconscious and propelling you towards your goals. By clearly defining your desires, eliminating distractions, and taking consistent action, you send a clear and unwavering message to your subconscious. This, in turn, ignites its immense potential for manifestation.

Remember, the journey towards your goals is a continuous process of refinement. As you progress, your vision may evolve, and your roadmap may need adjustments. Embrace this flexibility, but always maintain a core sense of definiteness. With unwavering belief, a clear vision, and consistent action, you can harness the immense power of your subconscious and transform your wildest dreams into reality.

The Power of Community: Amplifying Definiteness Through Shared Vision

Definiteness is a powerful force, but it can be further amplified by surrounding yourself with a supportive community. Sharing your vision and goals with others who resonate with them creates a synergy that strengthens your own unwavering belief.

Accountability Partners: Find a friend or colleague with similar goals and hold each other accountable for taking consistent action. Sharing your progress and challenges with someone who understands your journey can be incredibly empowering.

Mentorship: Seek guidance from individuals who have achieved success in your chosen field. Their insights and experiences can provide invaluable guidance and reignite your definiteness during challenging times.

Supportive Groups: Look for online forums, workshops, or mastermind groups focused on personal development and goal achievement. Being part of a supportive community of like-minded individuals can provide a sense of belonging, fuel your motivation, and expose you to new ideas and strategies that can further refine your definiteness.

Remember, your support system doesn't have to be limited to people you know personally. Inspirational books, podcasts, and documentaries can also play a vital role in keeping you focused on your goals and strengthening your definiteness.

A Final Word on Definiteness

Definiteness is a lifelong journey, not a one-time event. As you encounter challenges and setbacks, revisit your vision, reaffirm your commitment, and adjust your roadmap as needed. Remember, the power of definiteness lies in its consistency. By consistently focusing on your goals, taking action, and cultivating a growth mindset, you create a powerful synergy between your conscious mind and your subconscious, paving the way for the manifestation of your dreams.

Embrace the power of definiteness, and watch as your subconscious transforms from a vast, untapped potential into your most potent ally on the path to achieving your greatest desires.

Chapter 8 Willing Your Subconscious Into Unstoppable Action

"The difference between ordinary and extraordinary is that little extra." - Jimmy Johnson.

The seeds of our desires are planted within the fertile ground of the subconscious. But simply planting those seeds isn't enough. To transform them into a bountiful harvest, we need the unwavering force of persistence – the relentless pursuit of our goals in the face of obstacles and setbacks. This chapter delves into the power of persistence as the fuel that propels the subconscious from passive desire to unstoppable action.

Persistence: The Engine that Drives Your Subconscious

Our subconscious mind thrives on consistency. When we consistently focus on our goals and take action towards them, no matter how small, we send a powerful message to our subconscious. This persistent effort fuels the manifestation engine, propelling us closer to our desires.

Imagine a car with a full tank of gas. The potential for movement is there, but without a driver who persistently presses the accelerator, the car remains stationary. Persistence is the driver in this metaphor, urging your subconscious mind to take action and translate your desires into reality.

The Science of Persistence

Beyond anecdotal evidence, science supports the transformative power of persistence. Neuroplasticity, the brain's ability to change and adapt throughout life, plays a crucial role in this process.

When we consistently engage in a particular activity or focus on a specific goal, the neural pathways associated with that activity become stronger. Persistence strengthens these pathways within your subconscious, making the desired behaviour or outcome more ingrained and automatic.

J.K. Rowling: Persevering Through Poverty by Feeding the Subconscious

J.K. Rowling's journey to becoming a literary phenomenon is a testament to the power of persistence. A single mother facing poverty, Rowling poured her heart and soul into writing the Harry Potter series. Despite countless rejections from publishers, she persisted, fueled by a relentless belief in her story.

Rowling's unwavering persistence wasn't just about external actions; it was also about feeding her subconscious with unwavering belief. Despite the rejections, she continued to visualise success, refine her manuscript, and hold onto the unwavering belief that her story would one day find its audience. This relentless mental focus, coupled with consistent action, sent a powerful message to her subconscious, ultimately leading to the global phenomenon that is Harry Potter.

"It is not the mountain we conquer, but ourselves." - Edmund Hillary.

Rowling's story underscores the importance of aligning your conscious actions with unwavering belief. Persistence isn't just about doggedly pushing forward; it's about infusing your actions with a deep-seated conviction in your ability to achieve your goals.

Overcoming the Fear of Criticism: Aligning the Subconscious with Your Goals

The path towards your goals will inevitably involve criticism. There will be doubters who question your vision and naysayers who try to discourage you. These external voices can create dissonance within your subconscious, hindering your progress.

Building a Shield Against Criticism

To counter the effects of criticism, it's crucial to cultivate a shield against negativity. Here are some strategies to protect your subconscious from the damaging effects of doubt:

Identify Your Core Values: Remind yourself of your core values and why your goals are important to you. When negativity arises, refocus on your "why" – the deeper purpose that fuels your passion and perseverance.

Limit Contact with Negativity: Surround yourself with positive and supportive individuals who believe in you and your dreams. Minimise contact with those who constantly criticise and dampen your enthusiasm.

Reframe Criticism as Feedback: Not all criticism is meant to be malicious. Learn to discern constructive criticism that can help you improve from negativity meant to pull you down.

"The only person you are destined to become is the person you decide to be." - Ralph Waldo Emerson.

By cultivating a mental shield against negativity, you ensure that your subconscious receives a clear and unwavering message – a message of belief in yourself and your ability to achieve your goals.

Persistence Through Failure: Embracing Setbacks as Stepping Stones

The road to success is rarely paved with uninterrupted progress. Setbacks and failures are inevitable parts of the journey. However, by viewing these setbacks as opportunities for learning and growth, you can strengthen your resilience and emerge even stronger.

"Our greatest glory is not in never falling, but in rising every time we fall." - Nelson Mandela.

Here are some strategies for turning setbacks into stepping stones for your subconscious:

Analyse the Situation: Don't let setbacks become roadblocks. Take time to analyse what went wrong. Identify areas where you can improve and adjust your approach accordingly.

Maintain a Positive Focus: Dwelling on negativity only hinders your progress. Instead of focusing on the setback, focus on the lessons learned and the opportunities for growth.

Celebrate Small Victories: The path to success is paved with small wins. Celebrate your milestones, no matter how small, to maintain motivation and reinforce the positive momentum within your subconscious.

Persistence in Action: Inspiring Examples of Unwavering Will

History is filled with stories of individuals who harnessed the power of persistence to achieve remarkable feats. Here are a few inspiring examples:

Michelle Obama: Before becoming the first African American First Lady of the United States, Michelle Obama faced numerous challenges and rejections. After graduating from Princeton University, she struggled to find a job in corporate law due to firms' reluctance to hire African American graduates. Undeterred, she persisted in her pursuit of excellence, eventually becoming an associate at a prestigious law firm. Her unwavering determination and resilience in the face of adversity paved the way for her remarkable journey, which included roles as an advocate for healthy families, service members, and higher education.

Walt Disney: As mentioned in the previous chapter, Walt Disney faced countless rejections before achieving his dream of creating an animation empire. His unwavering persistence, fueled by a clear vision and unwavering belief, ultimately led to the creation of Mickey Mouse and the global phenomenon that is Disney.

These stories illustrate the transformative power of persistence. When you consistently focus on your goals, take action despite setbacks, and cultivate a shield against negativity, you send a powerful message to your subconscious. This message fuels your inner fire and propels you toward the manifestation of your desires.

Developing a Persistence Mindset

Cultivating a persistent mindset is key to aligning your subconscious with your goals. Here are some strategies to develop this mindset:

Focus on Progress, Not Perfection: Striving for perfection can lead to procrastination and discouragement. Instead, focus on making consistent progress, no matter how small. Celebrate your forward movement and trust the power of compounding efforts over time.

Develop Grit: Grit is the unshakeable resolve to persevere despite challenges. There will be days when you feel like giving up. Develop the mental fortitude to push through these moments and keep moving forward.

Visualise Success: Regularly engage in visualisation exercises where you see yourself achieving your goals. Immerse yourself in the positive emotions associated with success. The more vivid your visualisation, the stronger the message you send to your subconscious, reinforcing your belief in your ability to achieve your dreams.

"The only way to do great work is to love what you do. If you haven't found it yet, keep looking. Don't settle." - Steve Jobs.

Remember, developing a persistent mindset is a continuous effort. There will be days when doubt creeps in and motivation wanes. Be kind to yourself during these times. Remind yourself of your "why," refocus on your vision, and take consistent action, even if it's just a small step forward. Every step you take, every obstacle you overcome, strengthens the message to your subconscious, propelling you closer to your goals.

The Power of Habit

Persistence is closely linked to the concept of habit formation. Habits are ingrained behavioural patterns that become automatic over time. For example, brushing your teeth every morning or locking the door before leaving your house requires minimal conscious effort because they have become ingrained habits.

The power of habit lies in its ability to automate behaviour, freeing up your conscious mind for more complex tasks. By consistently taking small actions toward your goals, you can cultivate habits that support your long-term vision. These habits, fueled by the power of persistence, become ingrained within your subconscious, propelling you forward even on autopilot.

Remember, small, consistent actions repeated daily have a profound cumulative effect. Imagine trying to chip away at a large boulder with a hammer. A single swing might make a negligible difference. But with persistent, daily blows, even the most daunting obstacle will eventually crumble.

Here's how you can leverage the power of habit to support your goals:

Identify Key Actions: Break down your larger goals into smaller, manageable steps. These steps should be specific, measurable, achievable, relevant, and time-bound (SMART).
Focus on Consistency: Aim for consistent action, even if it's just for a short period each day. The key is to create a routine that becomes ingrained in your subconscious.

Track Your Progress: Monitor your progress to stay motivated. Seeing your forward momentum reinforces the positive feedback loop within your subconscious and strengthens your persistence.

By integrating these strategies, you can harness the power of habit to work for you, not against you. Persistence becomes less about sheer willpower and more about a natural flow of action fueled by the subconscious programming created by your consistent efforts.

Conclusion: The Unstoppable Power of Persistence

Persistence is a cornerstone of success. By consistently feeding your subconscious with unwavering belief, taking action despite setbacks, and cultivating a growth mindset, you ignite an unstoppable force within yourself. This force, fueled by persistence, propels you towards manifesting your dreams and empowers you to transform your desires into reality.

Remember, the journey towards your goals is a marathon, not a sprint. Embrace the process, celebrate the small victories, and never lose sight of your vision. With unwavering persistence, you can accomplish anything you set your mind to and unlock the limitless potential that lies within your subconscious.

Chapter 9 Amplifying Subconscious Power Through Synergy

"None of us is as smart as all of us." - Ken Blanchard.

The human mind is a vast reservoir of potential. Yet, within this vastness lies an even greater power – the power of synergy. Synergy, in its simplest form, refers to the interaction of two or more elements that produce a greater effect than the sum of their individual parts. This principle extends to the realm of the subconscious as well. By collaborating with others who share similar goals and visions, we can harness the collective power of our subconscious minds, propelling us towards unimaginable heights of achievement.

The Master Mind Principle and Coordinating Subconscious Efforts

In the previous chapter, we explored the transformative power of persistence in fueling individual subconscious action. This chapter delves deeper, exploring the concept of the Master Mind principle, introduced by Napoleon Hill in his book "Think and Grow Rich."

Hill defines the Mastermind principle as **"the coordination of knowledge and effort, in a spirit of harmony, between two or more people for the attainment of a definite purpose."** When individuals with aligned goals and unwavering beliefs come together in a spirit of collaboration, they create a powerful synergy that amplifies the subconscious power of each member.

Imagine two tuning forks, each vibrating at a specific frequency. When struck independently, they produce individual sounds. However, when held close together, the vibrations from one tuning fork influence the other, causing them to synchronize and produce a stronger, more unified sound. Similarly, when individuals with focused subconscious minds collaborate, a form of **"subconscious synchronization"** occurs. Their shared beliefs, visions, and unwavering focus create a powerful synergy that amplifies the subconscious potential of each member, propelling them toward a shared success that may not have been achievable individually.

The Wright Brothers: Collaborating to Multiply the Force of Their Subconscious

The story of the Wright Brothers exemplifies the power of the Mastermind principle. Wilbur and Orville Wright, two brothers with a shared passion for flight, dedicated years to researching, designing, and testing airplanes. Despite numerous setbacks and failures, their unwavering belief in their dream and their collaborative spirit fueled their persistence.

Their shared vision and unwavering belief in the possibility of flight created a powerful subconscious synergy. Each brother's individual knowledge, skills, and experiences complemented the other. They shared ideas, debated challenges, and offered mutual encouragement, all contributing to a unified subconscious force that ultimately led them to achieve the seemingly impossible – powered flight.

Creating an Invisible, Intangible Force by Harmonizing Subconscious Minds

The Mastermind principle transcends the physical realm. While collaborating in person can be highly beneficial, the power of synergy can also be harnessed through online communities, mastermind groups, or even simply by surrounding yourself with individuals who share your vision and values.

Here are some key aspects of creating a successful Mastermind group or collaborative environment to amplify subconscious power:

Shared Vision and Goals: The foundation of a powerful Mastermind is a shared vision and set of goals. Each member should be committed to a common purpose and inspired by the collective energy of the group.

Mutual Respect and Trust: A successful Mastermind thrives on open communication, mutual respect, and trust. Members should feel comfortable sharing their ideas, challenges, and vulnerabilities without fear of judgment.

Complementary Skills and Expertise: By bringing together individuals with diverse skills and experiences, the Mastermind creates a well-rounded support system. Each member can learn from and leverage the strengths of others, further amplifying the collective subconscious power.

Beyond Accountability: Building Psychological Safety

While accountability is a crucial element within a Mastermind group, the concept of psychological safety takes it a step further. Psychological safety refers to the feeling of being able to speak up, share ideas, and take risks without fear of negative consequences.

This sense of psychological safety fosters an environment where subconscious barriers are lowered. Members feel comfortable expressing vulnerabilities, exploring unconventional ideas, and seeking support without fear of judgment. This vulnerability becomes a catalyst for a deeper subconscious connection, further amplifying the group's synergy.

VERSES KINDLER PUBLICATION

The Law of Attraction: A Universal Force Supporting Synergy

The Mastermind principle aligns with the universal law of attraction, which posits that like attracts like. By surrounding yourself with individuals who share your vision and unwavering belief, you create a powerful vibration that attracts opportunities and resources that support your goals.

Imagine two tuning forks, one vibrating strongly and harmoniously and the other vibrating weakly and erratically. When placed close together, the strong vibrations influence the weaker fork, gradually aligning its frequency until they both vibrate in perfect unison. Similarly, surrounding yourself with individuals who embody the positive traits and unwavering belief you aspire to cultivate creates a powerful subconscious synergy. Their positive energy and unwavering belief act as a vibrational force, gradually aligning your own subconscious frequency with theirs. This alignment attracts opportunities and resources that resonate with your shared vision, accelerating your journey toward success.

The Subconscious Symphony: Harmonizing Beliefs and Emotions

Our subconscious minds are constantly picking up on subtle cues from our environment. When we surround ourselves with individuals who embody the positive traits and unwavering beliefs we aspire to cultivate, a subconscious "symphony" begins to play.

Imagine yourself joining an orchestra for the first time. Initially, your individual notes might sound discordant. However, as you practice and synchronize with your fellow musicians, a beautiful melody emerges. Similarly, collaborating with positive and focused individuals creates a harmonious subconscious environment. Their unwavering belief, positive affirmations, and enthusiastic energy subconsciously influence your internal state, reinforcing your positive beliefs and propelling you towards your goals.

The Power of Mirroring: Subconsciously Aligning Behaviors

Neuroscience sheds light on a fascinating phenomenon called mirroring. Mirroring occurs when we subconsciously mimic the behavior, mannerisms, and even emotions of those around us. This unconscious process plays a significant role in shaping our subconscious programming.

By surrounding yourself with individuals who consistently demonstrate the behaviors and work ethic aligned with your goals, you subconsciously begin to mirror these patterns. Their focused work ethic, positive self-talk, and unwavering belief become contagious, subtly influencing your own subconscious programming and propelling you to adopt similar behaviors that move you closer to your aspirations.

The Collective Unconscious: Tapping into a Reservoir of Shared Knowledge

Carl Jung, the renowned psychiatrist, introduced the concept of the collective unconscious – a vast reservoir of knowledge, memories, and archetypes shared by all humanity. When individuals with similar goals and visions collaborate, they create a synergy that taps into this collective wellspring of potential.

This synergy facilitates a form of subconscious communication. Ideas flow more effortlessly, solutions emerge seemingly out of thin air, and aha moments become more frequent. The group's collective focus amplifies the power of the collective unconscious, unveiling insights and solutions that may have remained hidden if pursued individually.

Building a Collaborative Mindset: Cultivating the "We" over the "Me"

To fully harness the power of synergy, cultivating a collaborative mindset is key. This mindset shifts the focus from individual achievement to the collective success of the group. Here are some strategies to foster this "we" over "me" mentality:

Celebrate Collective Wins: Recognize and celebrate the achievements of the entire group, not just individual members. This reinforces the sense of shared purpose and strengthens the bonds within the collaborative environment.

Practice Active Listening: Pay close attention to the ideas and perspectives of your collaborators. This not only fosters respect and trust but also allows you to tap into the collective wisdom of the group.

Embrace Open Communication: Be open to sharing your ideas, challenges, and vulnerabilities with your collaborators. This transparency fosters trust and allows others to offer support and guidance, further amplifying the collective subconscious force.

The Butterfly Effect: A Ripple of Synergy Across the Universe

The power of collaboration and its impact on subconscious power resonates with the concept of the butterfly effect. The butterfly effect, a cornerstone of chaos theory, suggests that small, seemingly insignificant actions can have profound and unforeseen consequences. In the context of collaboration, the synergy created by a group of individuals working towards a common goal can have a ripple effect, impacting not only their own success but also influencing the collective consciousness.

Imagine a pebble dropped into a still pond. The initial impact creates ripples that radiate outward, affecting the entire surface of the water. Similarly, the focused energy and unwavering belief generated by a collaborative group creates a ripple effect within the collective unconscious. This ripple effect can inspire others, attract opportunities, and shape the overall environment in ways that support the group's goals and ultimately benefit society as a whole.

Collaboration as a Catalyst for Social Change

Throughout history, collaboration has been a driving force behind social change. From the civil rights movement to the fight for environmental protection, groups of individuals with shared visions have come together to create a powerful synergy that has transformed the world.

Their unwavering belief, collective action, and the positive emotions generated through collaboration create a ripple effect that resonates with the collective unconscious. This synergy inspires others to join the cause, attracts resources and support, and ultimately leads to shifts in societal norms and behaviors.

Examples of Collaborative Ripples in Action

Consider the following historical examples of how collaboration created a ripple effect for positive social change:

The Abolitionist Movement: A network of abolitionists, through collaboration and unwavering belief, challenged the deeply ingrained institution of slavery. Their collective voice, fueled by emotional conviction, rippled across society, ultimately leading to the abolition of slavery in the United States.

The Women's Suffrage Movement: Through decades of collaboration, women's rights activists fought for the right to vote. Their unwavering belief and collective action inspired others to join the cause, creating a ripple effect that ultimately led to the passage of the 19th Amendment, granting women the right to vote.

The Environmental Movement: Collaboration between scientists, activists, and policymakers has been instrumental in raising awareness of environmental challenges. Their collective efforts created a ripple effect, influencing public opinion, government policies, and corporate practices toward a more sustainable future.

Harnessing the Power of Synergy for a Brighter Future

The potential for collaboration to amplify subconscious power and create positive change extends far beyond individual goals. By intentionally fostering collaborative environments across various sectors of society, we can create a synergy that addresses global challenges and paves the way for a brighter future.

Here are some areas where collaborative efforts can harness synergy for positive change:

Sustainability Initiatives: Collaboration between governments, businesses, and individuals can create a powerful force for environmental sustainability. Sharing knowledge, resources, and innovative solutions through synergy can accelerate the transition to a more sustainable future.

Global Health Initiatives: Combating global health challenges requires a collaborative approach. By synergizing the efforts of scientists, healthcare professionals, and NGOs, we can develop effective solutions, share resources, and create a healthier world for all.

Technological Innovation: Collaboration between researchers, entrepreneurs, and investors can amplify the subconscious potential for innovation. By synergizing their efforts, they can accelerate technological breakthroughs that address global challenges and improve everyone's quality of life.

A Symphony of Collaboration for Unstoppable Progress

The power of collaboration to amplify subconscious power is an undeniable force for good. By harnessing this synergy, we can not only achieve our individual goals but also contribute to creating a brighter future for ourselves and generations to come.

Remember, the universe thrives on connection and collaboration. By intentionally building bridges, fostering synergy, and aligning your goals with a collaborative environment, you tap into a reservoir of subconscious potential that propels you toward unstoppable progress. Let collaboration be the symphony that orchestrates your success and contributes to a better world for all.

Chapter 10 Channelling Emotion into Subconscious Drive

"The mind is everything. What do you think you will become." - Buddha

The human experience is a tapestry woven with threads of emotion. From the joyous highs of victory to the crushing lows of loss, our emotions colour our perception, guide our choices, and leave an indelible mark on our subconscious. But what if we could harness this emotional power, not just to react to the world, but to shape it? This chapter delves into the fascinating interplay between conscious emotion and subconscious drive, exploring how we can leverage the fire of our feelings to propel us toward our goals.

Leveraging Emotion to Influence Subconscious Thought and Behavior

Our subconscious mind acts as a silent conductor, orchestrating much of our daily behaviour and thought patterns. It stores deeply ingrained beliefs, habits, and emotional responses that often operate below the surface of our conscious awareness. Yet, the seeds of these subconscious programs are often sown by our conscious emotions.

Consider the feeling of excitement that bubbles up when you visualise yourself achieving a long-held dream. This emotional charge, when consistently experienced, can leave an imprint on your subconscious. Over time, the subconscious begins to associate the desired outcome with a positive emotional state, propelling you towards taking action that brings you closer to that dream.

This principle is beautifully captured by Dr. Joe Dispenza, a renowned neuroscientist, who states, **"When you change the way you feel on a consistent basis, you literally change the way your brain works on a cellular level."** By deliberately cultivating positive emotions associated with your goals, you can nudge your subconscious towards aligning your thoughts and behaviours to achieve them.

The Science Behind Emotional Influence on the Subconscious

The concept of emotions influencing the subconscious is backed by scientific evidence. Our brains are wired for emotional processing. The amygdala, a region deep within the brain, plays a crucial role in evaluating emotional stimuli and generating the physiological responses associated with those emotions. When emotions are triggered repeatedly, the amygdala strengthens the neural pathways associated with those emotions. This can create a feedback loop within the subconscious, making certain emotional responses more likely to occur in the future.

Furthermore, emotions can influence our decision-making processes. Studies have shown that emotions can activate specific areas of the prefrontal cortex, the region responsible for planning and executive function. This suggests that emotions can not only colour our perception of situations but also directly influence the choices we make. By consciously associating positive emotions with desired outcomes, we can prime our subconscious to make decisions that move us closer to those goals.

The Power of Negative Emotions: Fueling the Fire Within

While positive emotions are often touted for their motivational benefits, negative emotions can also play a crucial role in shaping subconscious drive. Feelings like frustration, anger, or fear can serve as powerful motivators when channelled constructively. Imagine a runner who feels frustrated with their current pace. This frustration can be a catalyst for pushing harder and striving for improvement.

The key lies in not allowing negative emotions to overwhelm us. Instead, we can use them as a springboard for positive action. By acknowledging the negative emotion and reframing it as a signal for change, we can harness its energy to fuel our motivation and propel us toward our goals.

For example, if you feel anxious about giving a presentation, acknowledge the anxiety and reframe it as excitement about the opportunity to share your knowledge. This reframing allows you to channel the nervous energy into a positive force that can enhance your performance.

Building Emotional Bridges: Practical Techniques

Now that we understand the power of emotions to shape our subconscious, how can we leverage this knowledge for success?

Here are some practical techniques you can employ:

Visualisation: Spend time each day vividly visualise yourself achieving your goals. Immerse yourself in the positive emotions associated with success – pride, accomplishment, joy. The more frequently you engage in this emotional visualisation, the stronger the connection between your desired outcome and positive emotions becomes in your subconscious.

Affirmations: Create positive affirmations that encapsulate your goals and desired emotions. Repeat these affirmations regularly, allowing them to sink into your subconscious and shape your mindset. For example, if your goal is to become a confident public speaker, an affirmation could be, **"I am a confident and compelling speaker who inspires and engages my audience."**

Emotional Anchoring: Pair a specific positive emotion with a physical action or object. For instance, squeeze a stress ball while visualising yourself achieving a goal and feeling a surge of accomplishment. Over time, the physical action (squeezing the stress ball) becomes an emotional anchor, triggering the associated feeling of accomplishment whenever performed.

Gratitude Practice: Cultivate an attitude of gratitude by regularly reflecting on the things you are grateful for. Gratitude fosters positive emotions and strengthens the neural pathways associated with those emotions in your subconscious. This is associated with those emotions in your subconscious. This positive foundation can bolster your resilience and fuel your drive towards achieving your goals.

Journaling: Journaling provides a powerful tool for exploring your emotions and identifying the emotional triggers that influence your behaviour. By reflecting on your emotional responses to situations, you can gain valuable insights into your subconscious patterns. Once you understand these patterns, you can begin to consciously shift them towards supporting your goals.

Beyoncé: Reframing Disappointment into Creative Fire

Beyoncé's career trajectory serves as a masterclass in harnessing emotions to fuel subconscious drive. While often portrayed as an invincible force, Beyoncé has spoken openly about the emotional challenges that have shaped her artistic journey.

A defining moment arrived early in her career with the disbanding of Destiny's Child, the immensely successful girl group that launched her into the spotlight. The heartbreak of this dissolution, a public and personal disappointment, could have easily derailed her ambitions. However, Beyoncé channelled this disappointment into a potent creative fire.

Drawing strength from the emotions associated with independence and artistic autonomy, Beyoncé embarked on a solo career. Her debut album, "Dangerously in Love," pulsated with a newfound power and confidence. Tracks like "Crazy in Love" and "Survivor" showcased a fiercer, more independent Beyoncé, a stark contrast to the persona she embodied within Destiny's Child.

This emotional transformation wasn't merely a performance; it seeped into her creative process. Beyoncé, now in control of her artistic vision, poured her emotions into her music. The frustration with limitations during her time in the group fueled a relentless pursuit of creative excellence. The desire to prove herself as a solo artist translated into meticulously crafted albums, electrifying live performances, and a relentless work ethic.

Building a Legacy Brick by Emotional Brick

Throughout her career, Beyoncé has continued to leverage emotions to shape her artistic direction. The immense pressure to maintain her superstar status could have easily become a source of creative stagnation. However, Beyoncé uses this pressure as a motivator, constantly pushing boundaries and defying expectations.

Her critically acclaimed visual album "Lemonade" serves as a prime example. The raw emotions surrounding love, betrayal, and, ultimately, forgiveness poured into this project resonated deeply with audiences. By confronting these complex emotions head-on, Beyoncé not only created a groundbreaking artistic statement but also reaffirmed her position as a creative force to be reckoned with.

The Power of Vulnerability

Significantly, Beyoncé's willingness to express vulnerability has played a crucial role in her emotional connection with her audience. By sharing her struggles and triumphs, she allows fans to see themselves reflected in her journey. This emotional connection fosters a sense of shared experience, further propelling her towards superstardom.

In conclusion, Beyoncé's story is a testament to the transformative power of emotions. By acknowledging, understanding, and channelling her emotions, she has not only navigated the challenges of a demanding career but has also transcended them. Her journey serves as an inspiration, demonstrating how we can all leverage the emotional wellspring within us to fuel our subconscious drive and achieve our full potential.

Emotions - The Fuel for Subconscious Drive, A Journey, Not a Destination

Our emotions are not simply fleeting experiences; they are the vibrant brushstrokes that paint the canvas of our subconscious. By consciously cultivating positive emotions associated with our goals and reframing negative emotions as catalysts for change, we can create a powerful subconscious current that propels us forward. However, it's crucial to remember that harnessing the power of emotions is a lifelong journey, not a one-time destination.

The subconscious is a vast and fertile ground, but like any garden, it requires constant care and attention. Planting the seeds of positive emotions and nurturing them with consistent practice is essential. We must cultivate a daily ritual of introspection, acknowledging our emotional responses and consciously shaping them towards supporting our goals. This might involve journaling to explore emotional triggers, practising gratitude to foster a foundation of positivity, or engaging in visualisation exercises to solidify the emotional connection with our desired outcomes.

Just as important as cultivating positive emotions is the ability to navigate negative emotions effectively. Ignoring or suppressing negative emotions can lead to emotional build-up and hinder progress. Instead, we can learn to reframe negative emotions as signals for change. Frustration can be a catalyst for seeking new solutions, fear can be an impetus for taking calculated risks, and anger can be channelled into assertive action.

The road to harnessing the power of emotions is not without its challenges. There will be setbacks, moments of self-doubt, and times when emotions threaten to overwhelm us. However, with consistent effort and a commitment to self-awareness, we can learn to navigate these challenges and emerge stronger.

Remember, the rewards are immense. By mastering the art of emotional intelligence, we can unlock the full potential of our subconscious. We can cultivate a life driven by purpose and propelled by unwavering motivation, a life where emotions become not obstacles but the very fuel that propels us toward achieving our wildest dreams.

Chapter 11 Accessing Your Subconscious Storehouse of Creative Power

"The unconscious mind is a vast reservoir of energy. When properly tapped, it can do wonders." - Milton Erickson, psychiatrist.

Imagine a hidden chamber within you, brimming with ideas, solutions, and boundless creativity. This, in essence, is the subconscious mind. Beyond the analytical chatter of the conscious mind lies a vast repository of experiences, emotions, and intuitive insights. While the conscious mind focuses on logic and reason, the subconscious operates on a deeper level, weaving connections, incubating ideas, and generating creative solutions that often surprise and astound us. This chapter delves into the power of the subconscious as a wellspring of creativity and explores techniques for unlocking its potential.

Understanding the Subconscious as a Vast Repository of Creative Potential

The subconscious mind acts as a silent observer, absorbing everything we experience – sights, sounds, emotions, and memories. These experiences don't simply vanish; they are stored within the intricate neural networks of the subconscious, forming a rich tapestry of knowledge and inspiration.

Think of a seasoned chef. Years of culinary experience have equipped them with a vast subconscious repertoire of flavours, techniques, and combinations. While consciously following a recipe, the chef might intuitively add a pinch of this or a dash of that, drawing from this subconscious wellspring to create a masterpiece. Similarly, the subconscious mind of a writer may unexpectedly generate a brilliant plot twist, or a poet crafts a poignant turn of phrase, all fueled by the vast reservoir of experiences and emotions stored within.

The Power of Dreams: Unveiling the Subconscious Canvas

Dreams, those enigmatic nocturnal journeys, offer a glimpse into the vibrant world of the subconscious. While often symbolic and seemingly nonsensical, dreams can be interpreted as messages from the subconscious, revealing creative solutions, hidden desires, or emotional blockages. By keeping a dream journal and reflecting on recurring themes or vivid imagery, we can begin to decipher the language of the subconscious and unlock its creative potential.

Aha! Moment: When the Subconscious Makes its Presence Known

Have you ever experienced the sudden flash of insight, the proverbial "Aha!" moment, that seemingly appears out of thin air? These moments of brilliance often stem from the subconscious mind. While we may be consciously grappling with a problem, the subconscious continues to work on it in the background, sifting through memories and experiences. Then, when the time is right, the subconscious presents its solution, a gift from the depths of our creative wellspring.

Howard Schultz: Visualising Success to Engage the Subconscious

Howard Schultz, the visionary behind Starbucks' transformation, serves as a compelling example of harnessing the subconscious for creative problem-solving. In his early days with Starbucks, Schultz dreamt of transforming the small Seattle coffee chain into a global phenomenon. However, achieving this vision required overcoming significant challenges.

To bridge the gap between his vision and reality, Schultz employed a powerful technique – visualisation. He spent time each day vividly picturing Starbucks cafes bustling with activity, customers enjoying their coffee, and the brand becoming a beloved household name. By consistently engaging his subconscious with this vision, Schultz not only fueled his own motivation but also began to attract the resources and partnerships necessary to turn his dream into a reality.

Schultz's story highlights the power of visualisation in tapping into the subconscious wellspring. By creating a clear mental image of your desired outcome and engaging your emotions in the process, you send a powerful message to your subconscious, setting it to work on finding solutions and propelling you towards your goals.

Techniques for Quieting the Conscious to Tap the Subconscious Wellspring

The constant chatter of the conscious mind can often drown out the subtle whispers of the subconscious. To access this wellspring of creativity, we need techniques to quiet the conscious mind and create a space for the subconscious to emerge.

Here are a few powerful practices:

Meditation: Meditation is a powerful tool for cultivating inner peace and reducing mental noise. By focusing your attention on the present moment and observing your thoughts without judgement, you create space for the subconscious to surface.

Mindfulness: Mindfulness practices, such as mindful walking or mindful eating, train you to be fully present in the moment. This quieting of the mind allows for a more direct connection with your subconscious intuition and creativity.

Freewriting: Freewriting involves writing continuously for a set period without stopping or editing. This stream-of-consciousness exercise bypasses the critical filter of the conscious mind, allowing subconscious thoughts and ideas to flow freely onto the page.

Sensory Deprivation: Techniques like spending time in a float tank or practising light deprivation can temporarily quiet the external stimuli that bombard our senses. This sensory deprivation can create a space for the subconscious to emerge and present its unique perspective and creative solutions.

Engaging the Arts: Artistic endeavours, whether painting, playing music, or dancing, can act as bridges to the subconscious. By engaging in these activities in a playful and non-judgmental way, we bypass the analytical mind and allow the subconscious to express itself freely, often leading to unexpected bursts of creativity.

The Power of Incubation: Letting Ideas Simmer in the Subconscious

Our journey to tap into the subconscious wellspring of creativity isn't always a linear process. Sometimes, the most powerful ideas don't emerge fully formed in a flash of inspiration. Instead, they require a period of incubation, a time when they simmer in the subconscious, undergoing a process of refinement and transformation.

Imagine a chef crafting a complex dish. The initial brainstorming might involve a multitude of ingredients and potential flavour combinations. However, before finalising the recipe, the chef might experiment with different variations, letting the flavours meld and mature. Similarly, the subconscious mind can benefit from a period of incubation for our creative ideas.

During this incubation period, the conscious mind may take a backseat, allowing the subconscious to work its magic. It sifts through the information and experiences we've exposed it to, drawing connections between seemingly disparate elements. This subconscious processing can lead to unexpected insights, innovative solutions, and a deeper understanding of the problem at hand.

The Spark of Intuition: When the Subconscious Takes the Lead

Intuition plays a crucial role in the creative process, serving as a bridge between the conscious and subconscious mind. It manifests as a gut feeling, a hunch, or a sudden flash of inspiration that seems to arise from nowhere. While often dismissed as mere guesswork, intuition is a powerful tool that can guide us toward creative solutions.

Think of a scientist on the verge of a breakthrough discovery. After years of meticulous research and data analysis, they might experience a sudden intuitive leap that unlocks a new perspective or reveals a missing piece of the puzzle. This intuitive nudge, fueled by the subconscious processing of information, can be the catalyst for a major scientific advancement.

Honing Your Intuition: Tuning into the Subconscious

While intuition is a powerful tool, it doesn't always speak in clear, concise language. Learning to recognize and trust your intuition requires practice and self-awareness.

Here are some ways to hone your intuition and bridge the gap between the conscious and subconscious:

Pay attention to your body: Our bodies often communicate with us through subtle cues. A tightening in the chest might signal a sense of unease about a particular direction, while a feeling of lightness could indicate you're on the right track. Learn to recognize these physical sensations associated with your intuition.

Practice mindfulness: Mindfulness exercises, like meditation, can help you become more attuned to your inner voice and the subtle messages your subconscious might be sending.

Keep a dream journal: As mentioned earlier, dreams offer valuable insights into the subconscious mind. By recording and reflecting on your dreams, you might uncover recurring themes or symbolic messages that can guide your intuition and inform your creative process.

Embrace experimentation: Don't be afraid to experiment with different approaches and ideas, even if they seem unconventional at first. The process of experimentation allows your subconscious to explore possibilities and can lead to unexpected breakthroughs.

Integrating the Conscious and Subconscious: The Dance of Creativity

The creative process is a beautiful dance between the conscious and subconscious minds. The conscious mind provides the focus, discipline, and critical thinking required to bring ideas to life. The subconscious, on the other hand, offers a wellspring of inspiration, intuition, and unconventional solutions. By fostering a healthy dialogue between these two aspects of our minds, we unlock our full creative potential.

Combining Techniques for Synergistic Effects

The most effective approach often involves a combination of these techniques. For instance, engaging in a mindful walk in nature can not only quiet the mind but also stimulate the senses with fresh air, sounds, and sights, fostering a connection with the subconscious. Following a mindful walk with a freewriting session can then allow the subconscious insights gleaned from the walk to flow freely onto the page.

Overcoming Creative Blocks: When the Subconscious Wellspring Runs Dry

Even the most creative individuals experience periods of stagnation, where the wellspring of inspiration seems to dry up.

Here are some strategies to overcome these creative blocks:

Stepping Away from the Problem: Sometimes, the most productive thing you can do is to step away from the problem altogether. Engaging in activities that bring you joy and relaxation can allow your subconscious to continue working on the problem in the background. Often, the solution will present itself unexpectedly when you least expect it.

Priming Your Subconscious: Expose yourself to diverse stimuli – read books in different genres, visit museums, and listen to new music. This variety of input can spark new connections in your subconscious, leading to fresh ideas and creative breakthroughs.

Collaboration: Working with others can be a powerful way to tap into the collective subconscious. Brainstorming sessions with colleagues or engaging in creative partnerships can spark new ideas and perspectives, reigniting the creative spark within you.

Unleashing the Creative Powerhouse Within - A Journey of Self-Discovery

The subconscious mind is not a passive reservoir; it's a dynamic wellspring that flourishes with exploration and intention. By understanding its potential, quieting the conscious mind, and employing the techniques outlined above, we embark on a lifelong journey of self-discovery, constantly uncovering new facets of our creative potential.

This journey is not without its challenges. There will be times when the creative flow seems to sputter, moments of self-doubt, and periods where the messages from the subconscious seem faint. However, with consistent practice and a commitment to nurturing your inner creativity, these obstacles can be overcome.

Remember, the rewards are immense. By unlocking the creative powerhouse within, you don't just generate innovative ideas or produce stunning works of art. You cultivate a more fulfilling and meaningful life. Creativity allows you to approach challenges with fresh perspectives, navigate life's uncertainties with a sense of resourcefulness, and experience the joy of bringing your unique vision to life.

Think of the countless artists, scientists, entrepreneurs, and everyday problem-solvers who have tapped into the power of their subconscious minds. Their contributions have not only enriched our world but also served as a testament to the transformative potential that lies within each of us.

So, embark on this adventure with an open mind and a playful spirit. Experiment with different techniques, embrace the unconventional and trust the whispers of your subconscious. As you delve deeper into this rich inner landscape, you'll not only unlock a wellspring of creativity but also discover a more authentic and empowered version of yourself.

Chapter 12 The Subconscious Broadcasting Station – Desire, Imagination, and Belief

"You may voluntarily plant in your subconscious mind any plan, thought, or purpose that you desire to translate into its physical or monetary equivalent. The subconscious acts first on the dominating desires that have been mixed with emotional feelings, such as faith"—Napoleon Hill.

Imagine your subconscious mind as a powerful radio transmitter, constantly broadcasting signals that shape your reality. These signals aren't random; they are fueled by your dominant thoughts, beliefs, and desires. This chapter delves into the profound influence of desire, imagination, and belief on the subconscious mind, exploring how we can consciously shape these signals to attract success and fulfilment.

The Subconscious: The Unsung Conductor of Our Lives

The subconscious mind, according to the dictionary, refers to the part of the mind that exists below the level of our conscious awareness. Yet, despite operating beneath the surface of our conscious thoughts, the subconscious exerts a powerful influence on our actions, behaviours, and, ultimately, the experiences we attract into our lives.

Think of a person consumed by negativity. Their subconscious, tuned to the frequency of negativity, filters experiences to confirm their pessimistic outlook. Opportunities might be overlooked, challenges magnified, and setbacks interpreted as proof that success is unattainable. Conversely, an individual brimming with optimism broadcasts a different signal. Their subconscious, tuned to the frequency of possibility, filters experiences through a lens of hope and resourcefulness. Challenges become opportunities for growth, setbacks provide valuable lessons, and opportunities are readily identified and seized.

This principle is beautifully captured by the Law of Attraction, a philosophy that suggests our thoughts and beliefs have the power to attract experiences that resonate with us. While the Law of Attraction has been met with some scepticism, its core concept—that our subconscious broadcasts shape our reality—aligns with the growing understanding of the mind-body connection.

Steve Jobs: Mastery of Engaging the Subconscious Through Desire, Imagination, and Belief

Steve Jobs, the visionary co-founder of Apple, serves as a compelling example of harnessing the power of the subconscious broadcasting station. Steve's unwavering belief in his vision, coupled with his vivid imagination and relentless desire to create revolutionary products, fueled his relentless pursuit of innovation.

The Power of Desire: Fueling the Creative Furnace

Steve's desire to create products that would "change the world" wasn't a fleeting sentiment but a burning passion that permeated his every thought and action. This powerful desire served as the foundation for his unwavering focus and determination. It propelled him through countless challenges, from securing funding for his early ventures to navigating the complexities of a competitive market.

The Magic of Imagination: Broadcasting a Future into Existence

Steves possessed a remarkable ability to envision the future. He didn't just dream of sleek computers and intuitive interfaces; he imagined them in meticulous detail, down to the user experience and the aesthetics. This vivid imagination allowed him to "broadcast" a clear picture of his desired reality to his subconscious mind, which then guided his actions and decisions towards achieving that vision.

The Strength of Belief: The Unshakeable Conviction

Steve's belief in his vision was unshakable. Even when faced with scepticism and doubt, he remained resolute, convinced of the transformative potential of his ideas. This unshakeable belief served as a powerful signal to his subconscious, reinforcing his commitment and empowering him to overcome seemingly insurmountable obstacles.

By harnessing the potent trio of desire, imagination, and belief, Steve Jobs transformed his vision from a dream into a reality. His story serves as a testament to the immense power we hold to shape our subconscious broadcasting station and, ultimately, our own destinies.

Discussion and Collaboration as Ways to Stimulate the Subconscious Mind

While the power of the subconscious broadcasting station lies within us, engaging in discussions and collaborating with others can play a significant role in stimulating and enriching the signals we transmit.

The Power of Shared Vision: Discussing your goals and aspirations with supportive individuals can amplify the signal of your desire. Hearing your vision articulated aloud by others can solidify it in your subconscious and bolster your belief in its attainability.

Collaboration as a Catalyst for Creativity: Brainstorming sessions with like-minded individuals can spark new ideas and perspectives, enriching the imaginative landscape of your subconscious. The collaborative process allows you to tap into the collective wellspring of creativity, leading to innovative solutions and approaches.

We are all connected to each other biologically. To the Earth, chemically. To the universe, atomically." - Neil deGrasse Tyson

Shaping Your Subconscious Broadcast: Practical Techniques

Understanding the power of the subconscious broadcasting station is only the first step. The true power lies in harnessing this knowledge to shape the signals we transmit consciously. Here are some practical techniques you can incorporate into your daily routine:

Reprogramming Your Subconscious Through Affirmations: Affirmations are positive statements that express your desired outcomes. By repeating affirmations regularly, you can begin to reprogram your subconscious mind, replacing limiting beliefs with empowering ones.

For instance, instead of the negative affirmation, "I'm not creative enough," replace it with the empowering affirmation, **"I am a creative and resourceful individual."** The key is to repeat these affirmations with conviction, believing in the possibility of your desired outcome.

Visualisation: Broadcasting Your Dreams into Reality

Visualisation is a powerful technique that involves creating a vivid mental image of your desired outcome. Engage all your senses in this visualisation – see yourself achieving your goal, feel the emotions associated with success, and hear the encouraging words of others. The more detailed and consistent your visualisation practice, the more effectively you can broadcast your dreams to your subconscious mind.

Gratitude: Tuning in to the Frequency of Abundance

Gratitude is a powerful antidote to negativity. By consciously focusing on the things you're grateful for, you shift the frequency of your subconscious broadcast towards abundance and positivity. Keeping a gratitude journal and reflecting on the blessings in your life each day can significantly impact the signals your subconscious transmits.

Mindfulness Meditation: Quieting the Static for Clear Transmission

The constant chatter of the conscious mind can interfere with the subtle messages of the subconscious. Mindfulness meditation helps quiet this mental noise, creating a space for the subconscious to emerge. By practising mindfulness regularly, you can enhance your ability to receive and interpret the messages your subconscious is broadcasting.

The Power of Repetition: Building Momentum for Change

Remember, shaping your subconscious broadcasting station is a marathon, not a sprint. Consistent effort and repetition are key to creating lasting change. By incorporating these techniques into your daily routine, you'll gradually reprogram your subconscious mind to broadcast signals that attract success, fulfilment, and the life you desire.

Discussion and Collaboration: Expanding Your Broadcast Range

While the power to shape your subconscious broadcasting station lies within you, don't underestimate the value of collaboration and discussion. Engaging with supportive individuals can amplify the impact of your efforts in several ways:

Accountability Partners: Sharing your goals and affirmations with a trusted friend or mentor can create a sense of accountability, keeping you motivated and on track with your subconscious reprogramming efforts.

Brainstorming and Feedback: Discussing your goals and challenges with others can spark new ideas and perspectives. The collective wisdom of a supportive group can help you identify blind spots and refine your vision, enriching the imaginative landscape you broadcast to your subconscious.

Celebrating Successes: Sharing your achievements with others amplifies the positive emotions associated with success. This emotional reinforcement strengthens the positive signals being broadcasted by your subconscious mind.

Our conscious mind is the conductor of a grand orchestra, setting the overall direction and making strategic decisions. On the other hand, the subconscious mind serves as the vast and powerful orchestra itself, capable of producing a symphony of experiences based on the signals it receives. By understanding the influence of desire, imagination, and belief on the subconscious broadcasting station and employing the above mentioned techniques, we can learn to conduct this symphony with intention. In doing so, we can harness the immense power of the subconscious mind to create a life that resonates with our deepest desires and aspirations.

Beyond the Individual Broadcast: The Collective Subconscious and the Power of Shared Beliefs

The concept of the subconscious broadcasting station extends beyond the individual. Just as our individual thoughts and beliefs shape our personal realities, collective beliefs, and cultural narratives can influence the experiences of entire communities and societies. This realm of shared consciousness, often called the collective subconscious, acts as a powerful transmitter, shaping the social fabric and influencing the course of history.

The Collective Subconscious: A Shared Tapestry of Beliefs

The collective subconscious is a complex concept, but it can be understood as a shared reservoir of beliefs, values, and assumptions that are passed down through generations, shaping the worldview of a particular culture or society. These shared beliefs can be positive or negative, influencing everything from social norms and economic systems to artistic expression and scientific advancements.

Examples of the Collective Subconscious in Action

Consider the concept of money. Our belief in the value of money isn't an inherent truth; it's a shared belief system within our society. This belief system allows money to function as a medium of exchange and fuels our economic engines.

Think about the fear of public speaking. While the physiological response to public speaking is rooted in biology, the underlying fear itself is often reinforced by cultural narratives that portray public speaking as an anxiety-inducing experience. This shared belief within the collective subconscious can perpetuate the very fear it reflects.

Harnessing the Power of the Collective Subconscious for Positive Change

The concept of the collective subconscious isn't deterministic. Just as negative beliefs can hold us back, shared positive beliefs can propel us forward. Social movements and cultural shifts often begin with a change in the collective subconscious. When a critical mass of individuals begin to question limiting beliefs and embrace empowering narratives, a ripple effect occurs, paving the way for positive societal transformation.

The Responsibility of the Individual Broadcaster

While the collective subconscious is a powerful force, it doesn't negate the importance of individual agency. Each of us has the responsibility to be a mindful broadcaster within the vast network of the collective subconscious. By consciously cultivating positive beliefs, challenging limiting narratives, and advocating for progress, we can contribute to a more positive and empowering collective broadcast.

Our understanding of the subconscious mind is constantly evolving. The concept of the subconscious broadcasting station, both on an individual and collective level, offers a powerful framework for understanding how our thoughts, beliefs, and desires shape our realities. By harnessing the power of conscious intention and mindful broadcasting, we can create a life – and a world – that resonates with our deepest aspirations.

The Power of the Subconscious Broadcast - A Call to Awareness

The human mind is a magnificent and complex instrument. The conscious mind, with its analytical prowess, allows us to navigate the world and make informed decisions. The subconscious mind, with its vast reservoir of experiences and boundless creativity, fuels our intuition and shapes our reality through the "subconscious broadcasting station."

Understanding the influence of desire, imagination, and belief on this internal broadcast system empowers us to take charge of our lives. By consciously shaping the signals we transmit, we can cultivate a mindset for success, attract opportunities, and foster an environment conducive to achieving our goals.

The greatest discovery of all time is that a person can change his future by merely changing his attitude." — Oprah Winfrey.

However, the power of the subconscious broadcast extends beyond the individual. We are all interconnected, and the collective beliefs and narratives we share shape the world around us. By becoming mindful broadcasters within the network of the collective subconscious, we have the potential to create positive change that ripples outward, impacting communities and societies as a whole.

The journey to mastering the subconscious broadcasting station is a lifelong pursuit. It requires dedication, self-awareness, and a commitment to continuous learning. Yet, the rewards are immense. By embracing the power of your subconscious mind, you unlock a wellspring of creativity, resilience, and the ability to shape your destiny. So, embark on this exploration with an open mind, a hopeful heart, and a willingness to become a conscious co-creator of your reality – both as an individual and as a contributing member of the collective human story.

Chapter 13 Intuition as the Bridge to Higher Consciousness

"Intuition is the whisper of the soul." - Rumi, Persian poet.

Intuition is often dismissed as a hunch or a gut feeling, a mere subjective experience with little practical value. However, a growing body of evidence suggests that intuition is a powerful tool that can connect us to a deeper wellspring of knowledge and understanding – a bridge to a state of higher consciousness. This chapter delves into the nature of intuition, explores how it arises from the subconscious mind, and offers strategies for developing our intuitive capacity.

Developing Intuition to Access Universal Intelligence through the Subconscious

Intuition transcends the limitations of our rational mind. It bypasses the need for linear analysis and taps into a more holistic understanding of the world around us. This deeper knowing often emerges as a sudden insight, a flash of inspiration, or a gut feeling that seems to arise from nowhere.

The source of intuition lies within the vast realm of the subconscious mind. Our subconscious acts as a vast repository of experiences, emotions, and information gathered throughout our lives. While much of this information remains below the surface of our conscious awareness, it continues to influence our thoughts, behaviours, and, ultimately, our intuition.

Think of an iceberg. The conscious mind represents the tip of the iceberg, the small visible portion. However, the vast majority of the iceberg – the subconscious mind – lies hidden beneath the surface. Intuition acts as a bridge between these two realms, allowing us to access the wisdom and insights stored within the depths of our subconscious.

The Role of Universal Intelligence:

Many believe that intuition connects us not just to our own subconscious mind but also to a broader field of universal intelligence. This concept, often referred to as the Akashic Records or the collective unconscious, suggests that a vast pool of knowledge and information exists beyond the individual mind. Intuition, then, serves as a conduit, allowing us to tap into this universal intelligence and gain insights that transcend our limited perspectives.

"The intuitive mind is a sacred gift, and the rational mind is a faithful servant. We have created a society that honours the servant and has forgotten the gift." - Albert Einstein.

While science has yet to prove universal intelligence, the power of intuition is undeniable. Countless historical figures, inventors, and artists have attributed their breakthroughs and creative leaps to flashes of intuitive insight.

Visionaries: Doug Williams Tapping into Subconscious Intuition

Doug Williams, a former professional football player and the first Black quarterback to win a Super Bowl, serves as a compelling example of the power of intuition. Throughout his career, Williams faced numerous challenges, including racial prejudice and scepticism about his abilities. However, he consistently relied on his intuition to guide him through difficult decisions.

"I always felt like I had a sixth sense on the field. It was like something was telling me exactly what to do." - Doug Williams.

In Super Bowl XXII, facing heavy underdog status, Williams led his team, the Washington Redskins, to a historic victory. He credits his success not just to his physical skills but also to his ability to trust his intuition and make split-second decisions based on gut feelings.

Williams' story highlights the practical applications of intuition. Intuition isn't just about mystical experiences; it can be a valuable tool for navigating complex decisions, solving problems, and achieving success in various aspects of life.

Integrating the Conscious and the Subconscious: Cultivating Your Intuitive Knowing

While intuition is a natural human capacity, our fast-paced, logic-driven world can often drown out its subtle whispers. The key to cultivating your intuitive knowledge lies in fostering a connection between your conscious and subconscious minds. Here are some strategies you can incorporate into your daily practice:

Quieting the Mind: Meditation and mindfulness practices help to quiet the constant chatter of the conscious mind, creating space for the subtle messages of your intuition to emerge.

Journaling: Regular journaling allows you to explore your thoughts, feelings, and recurring patterns. Over time, you may identify themes and insights that reveal the deeper wisdom of your subconscious mind.

Paying Attention to Dreams: Dreams offer valuable insights into the subconscious mind. Keeping a dream journal and reflecting on the symbolism within your dreams can help you unlock intuitive messages.

Embracing Body Awareness: Intuition often manifests as physical sensations – a tightening in the chest, a feeling of lightness, or a nudge in a particular direction. Tuning into your body's subtle cues can help you decipher the intuitive messages your subconscious is sending.

Openness to Synchronicity: Synchronicity refers to the meaningful coincidence of events. Paying attention to these synchronicities – seeing recurring numbers encountering the same symbol repeatedly – can be a way in which your intuition guides you towards opportunities or insights.

Overcoming Obstacles to Intuition: The Skeptic's Guide

Despite the growing appreciation for intuition, some individuals remain sceptical of its validity. Here are some common obstacles to developing your intuitive capacity and how to address them:

The Cult of Rationality: Western culture often emphasises logic and reason as the primary means of acquiring knowledge. This can lead to dismissing intuition as subjective or unreliable.

Remember: Intuition isn't a replacement for rational thought; it's a complementary tool. By integrating both logic and intuition, we gain a more holistic understanding of the world around us.

Fear of Being Wrong: Our fear of making mistakes can lead us to ignore intuitive insights, especially when they contradict prevailing logic.

Challenge Yourself: View intuition as an experiment. Start small by paying attention to your gut feelings in everyday situations. Over time, you'll gain confidence in your intuitive discernment.

Difficulty Interpreting Subtle Cues: Intuition often speaks in a language of subtle feelings, hunches, and fleeting impressions. Learning to decipher these cues requires practice and patience.

Develop a Discernment Practice: Reflect on instances where your intuition has proven accurate. Identify the specific feelings or sensations associated with those experiences. This will help you refine your ability to recognize intuitive insights in the future.

Intuition and the Path to Higher Consciousness

Intuition is more than just a gut feeling; it's a bridge to a deeper state of consciousness. By cultivating our intuitive capacity, we connect with a wellspring of wisdom that transcends the limitations of the ego. This expanded awareness allows us to:

Access Creativity: Intuition often fuels creative breakthroughs. By tapping into the vast reservoir of knowledge within the subconscious, artists, inventors, and problem-solvers can access unconventional solutions and innovative ideas.

Embrace Synchronicity: When we are attuned to our intuition, we become more aware of the meaningful coincidences and connections that surround us. This heightened awareness allows us to synchronise our actions with the flow of the universe, leading to a sense of purpose and fulfilment.

Develop Compassion: Intuition can foster empathy and understanding for others. By accessing a deeper level of awareness, we can connect with the shared humanity that binds us all.

Live a More Authentic Life: Intuition guides us towards choices and actions that align with our core values and life purpose. By trusting our inner knowing, we can navigate life's challenges with greater clarity and purpose.

"The only true wisdom is in knowing you know nothing." - Socrates.

The pursuit of intuition is a lifelong journey of self-discovery. It requires a willingness to quiet the mind, embrace the unknown, and trust the whispers of the soul. As we cultivate our intuitive capacity, we embark on a path toward a higher state of consciousness, one that allows us to live a more meaningful and fulfilling life.

The Ethical Considerations of Intuition: Aligning with Your Highest Self

While intuition offers a powerful tool for navigating life's complexities, it's crucial to approach its guidance with ethical awareness. Intuition can be influenced by personal biases, unresolved emotional baggage, and even ego desires. Here's how to ensure your intuition is aligned with your highest self and guiding you toward positive action:

Self-Awareness is Key: Self-awareness is the foundation of ethical intuition. Engaging in practices like journaling, shadow work, and therapy can help you identify unconscious biases and limiting beliefs that might distort your intuitive messages.

Questioning Your Motives: Before acting on an intuitive nudge, take a moment to reflect on your motivations. Is your intuition guiding you toward a place of compassion and service, or is it fueled by fear, anger, or a desire for personal gain?

Aligning with Your Values: Consider your core values and principles. Does your intuition align with your commitment to honesty, integrity, and respect for others? If not, it might be a signal to pause and seek further clarity.

Seeking Confirmation: While intuition can be a powerful guide, it's not always foolproof. In crucial situations, it's wise to seek confirmation from trusted advisors or by gathering additional information before taking action.

"The difference between an ordinary man and an extraordinary man is not that one is free of fear. The extraordinary man is simply not controlled by his fear." - Miyamoto Musashi.

The Role of Intuition in Social Justice and Collective Progress:

Intuition isn't just a personal tool; it can also play a vital role in social justice movements and collective progress. History is filled with examples of individuals who, driven by a deep sense of right and wrong, challenged the status quo and advocated for positive change. These leaders, like Martin Luther King Jr. and Rosa Parks, likely relied heavily on their intuition to guide them through moments of uncertainty and danger.

Intuition can also serve as a collective force for positive change. Social movements often gain momentum when a critical mass of individuals experiences a shared sense of injustice or a collective intuition that a different future is possible. By trusting and acting on these intuitive nudges, we can contribute to a more just and equitable world.

Embracing the Symphony of Consciousness – A Dance Between Reason and Intuition

The human mind is a magnificent tapestry woven with threads of reason and intuition. Reason, with its analytical prowess, allows us to navigate the complexities of the external world, weigh evidence, and make informed decisions. Intuition, on the other hand, bridges the gap between the conscious and subconscious, offering a glimpse into a realm of deeper knowing. It speaks in whispers, in sudden flashes of insight, and in the language of gut feelings.

Embracing both these aspects of our being is the key to living a truly fulfilling life. Imagine a skilled conductor leading an orchestra. The conductor, representing reason, ensures that all the instruments—the analytical mind, emotional intelligence, and intuitive knowing—are playing their parts in harmony. The result is a beautiful symphony, a masterpiece that transcends the limitations of any single instrument.

Developing our intuition requires dedication and a willingness to step outside the comfort zone of pure logic. Here are some final thoughts to guide you on this journey:

Practice Makes Progress: Like any skill, intuition strengthens with practice. Pay attention to your gut feelings, keep a dream journal, and engage in activities that quiet the mind and allow the whispers of your soul to emerge.

Embrace the Unknown: Intuition often beckons us towards uncharted territory. Learn to trust the nudge in your heart, even when it seems to contradict the logical path. Sometimes, the greatest discoveries lie beyond the map.

Celebrate the Aha Moments: When your intuition leads you to a breakthrough, a creative solution, or a deeper understanding, take a moment to celebrate. These "aha" moments serve as positive reinforcement, encouraging you to trust your inner knowing in the future.

Learn from Mistakes: Even the most finely tuned intuition isn't infallible. There will be times when your gut feeling leads you astray. View these experiences as learning opportunities, refining your ability to discern true intuition from fleeting emotions or ego desires.

The journey of integrating reason and intuition is a lifelong exploration. As we learn to trust the whispers of our soul and navigate the world with both logic and a sense of deep knowing, we co-create a life filled with meaning, purpose, and the profound satisfaction of living in alignment with our highest selves. This journey isn't just about individual transformation; it's about contributing to a collective awakening. As more and more individuals cultivate their intuition and embrace a harmonious dance between reason and inner knowing, we pave the way for a brighter future for all – a future woven from the threads of collective wisdom, compassion, and the unwavering pursuit of a better world.

Chapter 14 Conquering Unaware Fears to Let Your Potential Soar

"The only person you are destined to become is the person you decide to be." - Ralph Waldo Emerson.

Fear is an undeniable aspect of the human experience. It serves an evolutionary purpose, keeping us safe from danger and prompting us to avoid potentially harmful situations. However, when fear operates on an unconscious level, it can become a formidable obstacle, hindering our growth and preventing us from reaching our full potential. This chapter delves into the nature of unconscious fears, explores how they take root in the subconscious mind and offers strategies for overcoming them.

The Unseen Enemy: Unveiling the Roots of Unconscious Fears

Unconscious fears are those that operate beneath the surface of our conscious awareness. They often stem from childhood experiences, past traumas, or societal conditioning. These experiences can leave emotional imprints on our subconscious, shaping our beliefs and behaviours without our conscious knowledge.

For example, a child who experiences public humiliation during a school presentation might develop an unconscious fear of public speaking. This fear may manifest as anxiety, sweaty palms, or a racing heart whenever they are faced with a situation that requires speaking in front of others. The individual might not even be aware of the root cause of this fear, simply experiencing the physical and emotional discomfort without understanding its origin.

The Grip of the Subconscious:

The subconscious mind acts like fertile ground where seeds of fear can take root and grow. If left unchecked, these negative beliefs and limiting patterns can exert a powerful influence on our lives. They can manifest as self-doubt, procrastination, and a reluctance to step outside our comfort zones. Ultimately, they can prevent us from pursuing our dreams, achieving our goals, and living fulfilling lives.

"Our greatest fear is not that we are inadequate; our greatest fear is that we are powerful beyond measure. It is our light, not our darkness, that most frightens us." - Marianne Williamson.

Here's a breakdown of some common ways unconscious fears take root in the subconscious mind:

Negative Parental Messages: Critical or judgmental messages from parents during our formative years can embed limiting beliefs about our capabilities and self-worth within the subconscious.

Traumatic Experiences: Childhood traumas, such as bullying, accidents, or neglect, can leave deep emotional scars that manifest as unconscious fears in adulthood.

Societal Conditioning: Societal expectations and cultural norms can generate fears of failure, rejection, or not fitting in, shaping our subconscious perceptions of the world.

The Case of Nelson Mandela:

Nelson Mandela's life story serves as a powerful testament to the transformative power of overcoming unconscious fears. Imprisoned for 27 years for his fight against apartheid in South

VERSES KINDLER PUBLICATION

Africa, Mandela faced unimaginable hardships and uncertainties. However, he used his time in confinement for introspection and self-discovery. He confronted his own fears and cultivated a spirit of forgiveness and compassion. As he later stated:

"I learned that courage was not the absence of fear but the triumph over it. The brave man is not a man who does not feel afraid, but a man who conquers that fear" - Nelson Mandela.

By confronting his unconscious fears and fostering inner strength, Mandela emerged from prison as a beacon of hope and became a driving force for racial equality and reconciliation in South Africa. His story exemplifies the power of human resilience and the potential for personal transformation when we choose to confront and overcome our deepest fears.

Unearthing Your Hidden Fears: Strategies for Self-Discovery

The first step towards conquering unconscious fears is to bring them into the light of conscious awareness. Here are some strategies you can incorporate into your self-discovery journey:

Shadow Work: Carl Jung's concept of the shadow refers to the unconscious aspects of our personality that we repress or deny. Engaging in shadow work practices, such as journaling prompts or dream analysis, can help you unearth hidden fears and limiting beliefs stored within the subconscious mind.

Body Awareness: Our bodies often hold onto the imprints of past traumas and unresolved fears. Practices like mindfulness meditation, yoga, or somatic therapy can help you tune into your physical sensations and identify areas of tension or discomfort that might be linked to unconscious fears.

111

Inner Child Work: Our inner child represents the part of us that holds onto childhood experiences and emotions. Exploring your inner child through guided meditations or journaling exercises can help you identify unconscious fears that stem from your formative years.

Hypnotherapy: Hypnotherapy can be a powerful tool for accessing the subconscious mind and uncovering the root causes of unconscious fears. A qualified hypnotherapist can guide you into a relaxed state and help you explore past experiences that might be contributing to your current fears.

"The unexamined life is not worth living." - Socrates.

Mind Control Through Self-Talk: Reprogramming Your Subconscious

Once you've identified your unconscious fears, it's time to take action. The good news is that the subconscious mind is malleable. Through a process of disciplined self-talk and positive affirmations, we can reprogram our subconscious beliefs and rewrite the narrative that governs our lives.

Here are some key principles to keep in mind:

Challenge Negative Thoughts: When you catch yourself engaging in negative self-talk, consciously challenge those thoughts. Replace them with empowering affirmations that focus on your strengths and capabilities.

Visualise Success: Visualisation is a powerful tool for programming the subconscious mind. Take time each day to vividly imagine yourself achieving your goals and overcoming your fears. Feel the emotions associated with success, and allow those positive feelings to take root within your subconscious.

Practice Gratitude: Gratitude has the power to shift our focus from what we lack to the abundance that already exists in our lives. By cultivating an attitude of gratitude, we create a more positive emotional state within the subconscious mind, which can weaken the hold of fear-based beliefs.

Positive Self-Hypnosis: Self-hypnosis techniques can be used to create positive suggestions for your subconscious mind. Record affirmations in your own voice and listen to them regularly, especially before sleep when your subconscious mind is more receptive to suggestions.

Celebrate Small Wins: As you begin to overcome your fears, take time to celebrate your victories, no matter how small. Acknowledging your progress reinforces positive change and motivates you to continue on your journey.

Building Resilience: Living Beyond Your Fears

Overcoming unconscious fears is not a one-time event; it's an ongoing process. There will be times when fear resurfaces, and that's okay. The key is to develop the resilience to face your fears head-on and move forward despite the discomfort.

Here are some strategies to build resilience and live a life beyond your fears:

Develop a Support System: Surround yourself with positive and supportive people who believe in you and your potential. A strong support system can provide encouragement and motivation when you're facing your fears.

Embrace Discomfort: Growth often happens outside our comfort zones. Challenge yourself to take small steps outside your comfort zone every day, even if it means facing a fear head-on. With each successful challenge, your confidence will grow, and your fear will diminish.

Practice Self-Compassion: Be kind to yourself throughout this process. Change takes time, and there will be setbacks along the way. Treat yourself with compassion and understanding, and celebrate your commitment to personal growth.

Focus on the Present Moment: Fear often thrives on worry about the future or regret about the past. By anchoring yourself in the present moment through mindfulness practices, you can reduce the power of fear and make choices from a place of empowerment.

"It is not the mountain we conquer, but ourselves." - Edmund Hillary.

Conquering unconscious fears is a liberating experience. By bringing these hidden fears into the light of conscious awareness, we gain the power to rewrite our internal narrative and unlock our full potential. The journey requires dedication, self-compassion, and a willingness to step outside our comfort zones. But the rewards are immense – a life filled with greater confidence, resilience, and the freedom to pursue our dreams without fear.

Embracing the Power Within: A Life Free from Unconscious Fears

Imagine a life where fear no longer dictates your choices. Imagine pursuing your passions with unwavering confidence, knowing that your inner landscape is a fertile ground for growth, not a breeding ground for anxieties. Overcoming unconscious fears is not just about achieving specific goals; it's about reclaiming your power and embracing the vast potential that lies dormant within you.

This journey of self-discovery isn't a solitary pursuit. As more and more individuals confront their hidden fears and choose to live authentically, we collectively create a ripple effect of positive change. In a world where fear is met with courage and self-doubt is replaced with self-belief, it becomes a world brimming with possibility.

Here are some final thoughts to guide you on your path toward a life free from unconscious fears:

Trust Your Intuition: Intuition can be a powerful ally in navigating the often murky waters of the subconscious mind. Pay attention to your gut feelings, dreams, and synchronistic occurrences that nudge you in the right direction. As you develop your intuition, it can become a valuable tool for identifying and overcoming unconscious fears.

Find Your Purpose: Living a life aligned with your core values and purpose provides a powerful sense of direction and motivation. When you know what truly matters to you, fear loses its ability to hold you back. Exploring your passions, volunteering for causes you care about, and fostering meaningful relationships can all contribute to discovering your life's purpose.

Embrace Forgiveness: Holding onto resentment and anger, particularly towards yourself, can create fertile ground for fear to flourish. Practice forgiveness, not just for others but also for yourself. Letting go of past hurts allows you to move forward with a lighter heart and a more open mind.

Celebrate the Journey: Overcoming unconscious fears is a lifelong adventure. There will be moments of triumph and moments of doubt. Celebrate your victories, big and small, and learn from your setbacks. The most important thing is to keep moving forward on your path toward self-discovery and personal empowerment.

"You gain strength, courage, and confidence by every experience in which you really stop to look fear in the face. You must do the thing you think you cannot do." - Eleanor Roosevelt.

Ultimately, conquering unconscious fears is about reclaiming your birthright – the right to live a life filled with passion, purpose, and unwavering belief in your own potential. It's about becoming the architect of your own destiny, empowered by self-awareness and guided by the unwavering light of your authentic self. As you embark on this transformative journey, remember you are not alone. We are all on this path together, creating a world where courage triumphs over fear and where the human spirit soars to ever-greater heights.

Beyond the Individual: The Ripple Effect of Unmasking Fear

Overcoming unconscious fears isn't just a personal victory; it has the potential to create a ripple effect of positive change that extends far beyond the individual. Here's how:

Collective Healing: As individuals confront and heal their own hidden fears, they contribute to a collective shift in consciousness. Fear thrives in isolation, but courage flourishes when shared. By openly discussing our struggles and celebrating our victories, we inspire others to embark on their own journeys of self-discovery, fostering a more courageous and compassionate society.

Empowering the Next Generation: When parents and caregivers have addressed their unconscious fears, they are better equipped to raise emotionally healthy children. By modelling courage, vulnerability, and self-compassion, we create a safe space for children to explore their emotions and develop a healthy relationship with fear. This, in turn, fosters a future generation empowered to face challenges head-on and create a more peaceful and just world.

Building Stronger Relationships: Unconscious fears can often hinder our ability to form and maintain healthy relationships. By confronting these fears, we become more open to connection, vulnerability, and trust. This allows us to build stronger relationships with loved ones, colleagues, and members of our community, fostering a more supportive and collaborative world.

Promoting Social Change: Many social injustices and societal ills stem from underlying fears – fear of the unknown, fear of difference, and fear of change. When individuals break free from the hold of their unconscious fears, they become more open-minded and empathetic, fostering a climate where social progress is possible. They are more likely to speak out against injustice, challenge the status quo, and advocate for positive change.

The Hero's Journey Within: A Call to Courage

The process of overcoming unconscious fears mirrors the archetypal hero's journey. We all have the potential to be the hero of our own stories, venturing into the unknown depths of our psyches to confront the dragons of fear that reside within. This journey requires courage, perseverance, and a willingness to face the darkness within ourselves. But the rewards are immense – a life of authenticity, purpose, and the unwavering belief in our ability to create positive change in the world.

Will you answer the call?

This chapter serves as a call to action, an invitation to embark on the transformative journey of confronting your unconscious fears. Remember, you are not alone on this path. There are countless resources available to guide you, from self-help books and online courses to therapists and support groups. The most important thing is to take the first step, acknowledge the power that fear may hold over you, and commit to a life lived with courage, authenticity, and unwavering belief in your potential.

As you embark on this journey, may you find the strength to confront your fears, the wisdom to navigate the unknown, and the courage to embrace the hero that lies dormant within you. Together, let us create a world where fear is no longer the master but where courage, compassion, and the unwavering pursuit of our highest potential pave the way for a brighter future for all.

Chapter 15 Conclusion – Realising the Vast Capabilities Uncovered

"The only limit to our realisation of tomorrow will be our doubts of today." - Franklin D. Roosevelt.

Throughout this exploration, we've delved into the fascinating realm of the subconscious mind, uncovering its profound influence on our thoughts, behaviours, and, ultimately, our potential for success and fulfilment. We've explored various techniques for harnessing the power of the subconscious, from cultivating intuition to overcoming unconscious fears. Now, as we reach the conclusion of this journey, let's revisit the key principles we've encountered and examine how they can empower you to unlock the vast capabilities that lie dormant within your subconscious.

Key Principles Revisited: Shaping the Subconscious Landscape

The Power of Suggestion: The subconscious mind is highly receptive to suggestion. By planting positive affirmations, visualising success, and surrounding yourself with inspiring messages, you can create a fertile ground for positive change within your subconscious.

The Role of Emotions: Emotions act as a bridge between the conscious and subconscious mind. Positive emotions like gratitude, joy, and excitement can empower the subconscious, while negative emotions like fear and anger can hinder their potential. Therefore, cultivating a positive emotional state is crucial for harnessing the power of the subconscious.

The Importance of Repetition: The subconscious mind thrives on repetition. By consistently engaging in practices like positive affirmations, visualisation, and guided meditations, you can reinforce desired beliefs and behaviours, shaping your subconscious landscape over time.

"We become what we think about all day long." - Earl Nightingale.

The Strength of Intention: Setting clear intentions for what you want to achieve is essential for programming your subconscious mind. When you have a well-defined goal and a strong desire to achieve it, you send a powerful message to your subconscious, activating its resources to support your journey.

The Language of the Subconscious: The subconscious mind responds more readily to imagery, emotions, and vivid language than to dry logic and reason. Therefore, incorporating visualisation, storytelling, and emotionally charged affirmations into your practices can enhance their effectiveness in influencing your subconscious.

The Power of the Present Moment: The subconscious mind operates in the present moment. By anchoring yourself in the present through mindfulness practices, you can release the hold of past regrets and anxieties that might be limiting your subconscious potential.

These are just some of the key principles that can guide you as you unlock the power of your subconscious mind. Remember, the subconscious is a vast and complex landscape, ever-evolving and responding to your thoughts, emotions, and actions. By applying these principles with dedication and consistency, you can cultivate a subconscious mind that supports your goals, fuels your creativity, and empowers you to live a life beyond your limitations.

Embracing the Inner Compass: Trusting the Subconscious for Inspired Action

The journey of harnessing the power of the subconscious mind isn't just about achieving specific goals; it's about cultivating a deep trust in your inner wisdom. The subconscious holds a vast reservoir of knowledge, experiences, and intuitive insights that can guide you toward a life of fulfilment. Here's how to tap into this inner compass and take inspired action:

Quiet the Mind: Meditation and mindfulness practices help to quiet the constant chatter of the conscious mind, creating space for the subtle whispers of your intuition to emerge. In the stillness, you can connect with the deeper knowing that resides within your subconscious.

Pay Attention to Dreams: Dreams offer valuable insights into the subconscious mind. Keeping a dream journal and reflecting on the symbolism within your dreams can help you uncover hidden desires, fears, and intuitive nudges from your subconscious.

Embrace Synchronicity: Synchronicity, the meaningful coincidence of events, can be a way in which your subconscious guides you towards opportunities or insights. Pay attention to these synchronicities—seeing recurring numbers or encountering the same symbol repeatedly—and trust that they might be pointing you in the right direction.

Notice Bodily Sensations: Our bodies often hold onto the imprints of subconscious messages. Tuning into your physical sensations – a tightening in the chest, a feeling of lightness, or a nudge in a particular direction – can help you decipher the messages your subconscious is sending.

"The intuitive mind is a sacred gift, and the rational mind is a faithful servant. We have created a society that honours the servant and has forgotten the gift." - Albert Einstein.

By developing a deeper connection with your subconscious and learning to trust its guidance, you can embark on a path of inspired action. Decisions that once felt overwhelming become clear, opportunities arise seemingly out of thin air, and your life unfolds with a sense of purpose and effortless flow.

A Parting Reflection: The Subconscious Mind – A Tapestry Yet to Be Fully Woven

As we conclude this exploration of the subconscious mind, it's important to acknowledge its enigmatic nature. Unlike the conscious mind, which operates with a linear logic, the subconscious is a realm of symbolism, emotions, and intuitive leaps. It's a constantly evolving tapestry woven from the threads of our experiences, beliefs, and deepest desires. While we've explored various techniques to influence and harness its power, the subconscious ultimately remains a mystery, a hidden wellspring of potential waiting to be further explored.

Here are some final considerations to ponder as you continue your journey of self-discovery:

The Paradox of Control: While we can influence the subconscious through deliberate practices, it's important to maintain a sense of respect for its autonomy. The subconscious mind has its own agenda, and sometimes, the most potent breakthroughs occur when we allow it to work its magic without forceful control. Trust the process, plant the seeds of intention, and allow your subconscious the space to orchestrate its own unique solutions. Imagine yourself as a gardener, nurturing the fertile ground of your subconscious but ultimately trusting the inherent wisdom of the seeds you've sown to sprout and blossom in your own time.

The Power of Unconscious Processing: The subconscious mind never sleeps. While we slumber, our subconscious continues to process information, make connections, and generate creative solutions. By incorporating practices like sleep affirmations or setting intentions before bed, we can tap into this powerful unconscious processing power and wake up to new insights and solutions. Think of sleep as a time for your subconscious mind to sift through the day's experiences, consolidate memories, and forge new connections. By planting the seeds of intention before you drift off, you can guide this unconscious processing and awaken to a harvest of fresh perspectives and creative ideas.

The Collective Subconscious: Just as we have individual subconscious minds, some theorists propose the existence of a collective subconscious – a shared pool of knowledge, memories, and archetypes that transcends individual experience. While the concept remains controversial, it's an intriguing idea that suggests our subconscious minds might be interconnected in ways we don't yet fully understand. Imagine the collective subconscious as a vast ocean of shared human experiences from which we all draw and contribute. By cultivating a sense of connection and empathy, we can tap into this collective wisdom and contribute to a more positive and harmonious collective unconscious for all.

The Ethical Considerations: As we delve deeper into the realm of the subconscious, it's crucial to consider the ethical implications. Techniques like subliminal messaging can be used to manipulate behaviour without conscious awareness. Therefore, it's important to approach these techniques with caution and prioritise using the power of the subconscious for personal empowerment and positive change. The subconscious mind is a powerful tool, and like any tool, it can be used for good or for ill. The responsibility lies with us to wield this power ethically and with the intention of creating a better world for ourselves and others.

"Until you make the unconscious conscious, it will direct your life, and you will call it fate." - Carl Jung.

In conclusion, the subconscious mind is a fascinating and ever-evolving frontier within us. By fostering a deeper connection with this inner world, we unlock a vast reservoir of potential, creativity, and intuitive wisdom. The journey of exploring the subconscious is a lifelong adventure filled with both challenges and profound discoveries. Remember, the key lies in approaching this exploration with an open mind, a sense of curiosity, and respect for the mystery that continues to unfold within us.

As you embark on your own journey of self-discovery, may you find the courage to delve into the depths of your subconscious, the wisdom to decipher its messages, and the trust to surrender to the transformative power that lies dormant within. The subconscious mind is a tapestry yet to be fully woven, and you, the artist, hold the brush. Let your intuition guide your strokes, and watch as your life unfolds in a masterpiece of purpose, fulfilment, and the boundless potential that resides within the depths of your being. Remember, the journey of the subconscious is not a solitary pursuit; it's a collaborative effort between your conscious mind and your inner wisdom. Embrace the dance between these two aspects of yourself, and together, create a life that transcends your limitations and expresses the full brilliance of who you truly are.

Verses Kindler Publication

Verses Kindler Publication

Reach us through our website -

https://www.verseskindlerpublication.com/

For more information visit our Instagram or Facebook page.